easy knitting
Country

easy knitting
Country

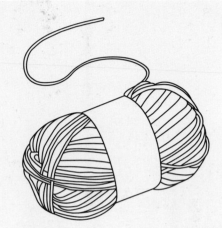

30 projects to make for your home and to wear

Consultant: Nikki Trench

hamlyn

An Hachette UK Company
www.hachette.co.uk

First published in Great Britain in 2013 by
Hamlyn, a division of Octopus Publishing Group Ltd
Endeavour House
189 Shaftesbury Avenue
London
WC2H 8JY
www.octopusbooks.co.uk

ISBN 978-0-600-62832-3

A CIP catalogue record for this book is available from the
British Library

Printed and bound in China

10 9 8 7 6 5 4 3 2 1

Contents

Introduction

If you can knit a few basic stitches, you can create stylish knitted items to wear, use to decorate your home and give as gifts for friends and family.

Whether you are a relative beginner, a confident convert or a long-term aficionado, there are projects here to delight. While your first attempts may be a bit uneven, a little practice and experimentation will ensure you soon improve. None of the projects here is beyond the scope of even those fairly new to the hobby.

Country style is perfect for crafts of all kinds and knitting is no exception. The projects in this book personify the charm and appeal of a rural lifestyle – even if it is only in your dreams. Knit gorgeous clothes, from scarves and socks to jackets and hats, or decorative and practical items for your home such as throws and egg cosies.

Knitting essentials

All you really need to get knitting is a pair of needles and some yarn. For some projects, that's it; for others additional items are required, most of which can be found in a fairly basic sewing kit. All measurements are given in metric and imperial. Choose which to work in and stick with it since conversions may not be exact.

- **Needles** These come in metric (mm), British and US sizes and are made from different materials, all of which affect the weight and 'feel' of the needles – which you choose is down to personal preference. Circular and double-pointed needles are sometimes used as well.
- **Yarns** Specific yarns are listed for each project, but full details of the yarn's composition and the ball lengths are given so that you can choose alternatives, either from online sources or from your local supplier, many of whom have very knowledgeable staff. Do keep any leftover yarns (not forgetting the ball bands, since these contain vital information) to use for future projects.
- **Additional items**: Some projects require making up and finishing, and need further materials or equipment, such as sewing needles, buttons and other accessories. These are detailed in each project's Getting Started box.

What is in this book

All projects are illustrated with several photographs to show you the detail of the work – both inspirational and useful for reference. A full summary of each project is given in the Getting Started box so you can see exactly what's involved. Here, projects are graded from one ball of yarn (straightforward, suitable for beginners) through two (more challenging) to three balls (for knitters with more confidence and experience).

Also in the Getting Started box is the size of each finished item, yarn(s), needles and additional items needed, and what tension/gauge the project is worked in. Finally, a breakdown of the steps involved is given so you know exactly what the project entails before you start.

At the beginning of the pattern instructions is a key to all abbreviations that are used in that project, while occasional notes expand on the pattern instructions where necessary.

If you have enjoyed the projects here, you may want to explore the other titles in the Easy Knitting series: *Babies & Children*, *Chic*, *Cosy*, *Vintage & Retro* and *Weekend*. For those who enjoy crochet, a sister series, Easy Crochet, features similarly stylish yet simple projects.

Metric	British	US
2 mm	14	0
2.5 mm	13	1
2.75 mm	12	2
3mm	11	n/a
3.25 mm	10	3
3.5 mm	n/a	4
3.75 mm	9	5
4 mm	8	6
4.5 mm	7	7
5 mm	6	8
5.5 mm	5	9
6 mm	4	10
6.5 mm	3	10.5
7 mm	2	n/a
7.5 mm	1	n/a
8 mm	0	11
9 mm	0	13
10 mm	0	15

Shawl-collared jacket

Snuggle up in this warm, practical jacket that's quick to knit and easy to wear.

This shaped jacket with a two-button fastening is knitted in chunky yarn and stocking/stockinette stitch with garter stitch trims and collar. The top section of the jacket, including the raglan armhole shaping, is worked all together as a yoke on a circular needle.

GETTING STARTED

Easy fabric to knit in basic stocking/stockinette stitch, but large number of stitches on yoke and shaping raglans need some expertise

Size:
To fit bust: 76–81[86–91:97–102:107–112] cm/30–32[34–36:38–40:42–44]in
Actual size: 96[108:120:132]cm/37½[42½:47:52]in
Length to shoulder: 56[59:62:66]cm/22[23¼:24½:26]in
Sleeve seam: 33[34:36:37]cm/13[13½:14:14½]in
Note: Figures in square brackets [ ] refer to larger sizes; where there is only one set of figures, it applies to all sizes

How much yarn:
11[13:15:17] x 50g (2oz) balls of Twilleys Freedom Wool, approx 50m (55 yards) per ball

Needles:
Pair of 8mm (no. 0/US 11) knitting needles
Pair of 10mm (no. 000/US 15) knitting needles
10mm (no. 000/US 15) circular knitting needle, 80cm (32in) long

Additional items:
2 large buttons
2 x safety pins, spare needle, stitch markers

Tension/gauge:
10 sts and 14 rows measure 10cm (4in) square over st st on 10mm (no. 000/US 15) needles
IT IS ESSENTIAL TO WORK TO THE STATED TENSION/GAUGE TO ACHIEVE SUCCESS

What you have to do:
Work in stocking/stockinette stitch. Shape side edges by decreasing and increasing. Use a circular needle (for large number of stitches) to work yoke in rows. Shape collar with turning rows.

The Yarn

Twilleys Freedom Wool is a 100% natural fibre with a loosely spun construction and super-soft touch. It is ideal for warm winter wear and is available in a good range of solid colours as well as some interesting variegated shades.

Instructions

Abbreviations:
alt = alternate; **beg** = beginning; **cont** = continue; **dec** = decrease(ing); **foll** = follow(s)(ing); **g st** = garter stitch (every row knit); **inc** = increase(ing); **k** = knit; **m1** = make a stitch by picking up bar between sts and knitting into back of it; **p** = purl; **rem** = remain; **rep** = repeat; **RS** = right side; **sl** = slip; **st(s)** = stitch(es); **st st** = stocking/stockinette stitch; **tbl** = through back of loop(s); **tog** = together; **WS** = wrong side; **yfwd** = yarn forward/yarn over

BACK:
With 8mm (no. 0/US 11) needles cast on 50[56:62:68] sts. K8 rows. Change to 10mm (no. 000/US 15) needles.
Dec row: (RS) K2, k2tog tbl, k to last 4 sts, k2tog, k2.
Beg with a p row, work 3[3:3:5] rows in st st.
Rep last 4[4:4:6] rows twice more, then work dec row again. 42[48:54:60] sts. Work 5[7:9:5] rows.
Inc row: (RS) K2, m1, k to last 2 sts, m1, k2.
Work 3 rows in st st.
Rep last 4 rows twice more, then work inc row again. 50[56:62:68] sts.
Work 7 rows in st st, ending with a p row.
Cut off yarn and leave sts on a spare needle.

SLEEVES:
With 8mm (no. 0/US 11) needles cast on 28[30:32:36] sts. K8 rows. Change to 10mm (no. 000/US 15) needles. Beg with a k row, work 2 rows in st st.
Inc row: (RS) K2, m1, k to last 2 sts, m1, k2.
Work 11 rows in st st.
Rep last 12 rows twice more, then work inc row again. 36[38:40:44] sts.
Work 1[3:5:7] rows in st st, ending with a p row.
Cut off yarn and leave sts on a spare needle.

LEFT FRONT:

With 8mm (no. 0/US 11) needles cast on 27[30:33:36] sts. K8 rows. Change to 10mm (no. 000/US 15) needles.

Dec row: (RS) K2, k2tog tbl, k to end.

Next row: K5, p to end. * Keeping front 5 sts in g st as set, work 2[2:2:4] rows in st st. Rep last 4[4:4:6] rows twice more, then work dec row again. 23[26:29:32] sts. Work 5[7:9:5] rows in st st.

Inc row: (RS) K2, m1, k to end. Work 3 rows straight. Rep last 4 rows twice more, then work inc row again. 27[30:33:36] sts. Work 7 rows straight, ending with a p row. * Cut off yarn and leave sts on a spare needle.

RIGHT FRONT:

With 8mm (no. 0/US 11) needles cast on 27[30:33:36] sts. K8 rows. Change to 10mm (no. 000/US 15) needles.

Dec row: (RS) K to last 4 sts, k2tog, k2.

Next row: P to last 5 sts, k5.

Work as Left front from * to * but reversing inc row, making 1st buttonhole on 25th[27th:29th:31st] row from beg and 2nd buttonhole on foll 18th row as foll:

Buttonhole row: (RS) K1, k2tog, yfwd, k to end.

Do not cut off yarn.

YOKE:

With 10mm (no. 000/US 15) circular needle and RS facing, work across all sts as foll:

Joining row: From right front k5 and sl these 5 sts on to safety-pin for collar, k to last 4 sts, k2tog, k2; from 1st sleeve k2, k2tog tbl, k to last 4 sts, k2tog, k2; from back k2, k2tog tbl, k to last 4 sts, k2tog, k2; from 2nd sleeve k2, k2tog tbl, k to last 4 sts, k2tog, k2; from left front k2, k2tog tbl, k to last 5 sts, turn and leave rem 5 sts on safety pin for collar. 158[174:190:210] sts. Work forwards and back in rows as foll:

Next row: (WS) P19[22:25:28], k4, p30[32:34:38], k4, p44[50:56:62], k4, p30[32:34:38], k4, p19[22:25:28]. The last row sets position of 4 sts in g st at raglans.

Next row: K23[26:29:32], k2tog tbl, k26[28:30:34], k2tog, k52[58:64:70], k2tog tbl, k26[28:30:34], k2tog, k23[26:29:32]. 154[170:186:206] sts.

Work 1 row straight as set.

1st and 2nd sizes only:

Next row: K2tog tbl, k15[18], k2tog, k4, k2tog tbl, k24[26], k2tog, k4, k2tog tbl, k40[46], k2tog, k4, k2tog tbl, k24[26], k2tog, k4, k2tog tbl, k15[18], k2tog. 144[160] sts. Work 1 row straight as set.

Next row: K21[24], k2tog tbl, k22[24], k2tog, k50[56], k2tog tbl, k22[24], k2tog, k21[24]. 140[156] sts. Work 1 row straight as set.

1st size only:

Next row: K2tog tbl, k13, k2tog, k4, k2tog tbl, k20, k2tog, k4, k2tog tbl, k38, k2tog, k4, k2tog tbl, k20, k2tog, k4, k2tog tbl, k13, k2tog. 130 sts. Work 1 row straight as set.

Next row: K19, k2tog tbl, k18, k2tog, k48, k2tog tbl, k18, k2tog, k19. 126 sts. Work 1 row straight as set.

All sizes:
Next row: K2tog tbl, k11[16:21:24], k2tog, k4, k2tog tbl, k16[22:28:32], k2tog, k4, k2tog tbl, k36[44:52:58], k2tog, k4, k2tog tbl, k16[22:28:32], k2tog, k4, k2tog tbl, k11[16:21:24], k2tog. 116[146:176:196] sts. Work 1 row straight as set.
Next row: K11[16:21:24], k2tog, k4, k2tog tbl, k14[20:26:30], k2tog, k4, k2tog tbl, k34[42:50:56], k2tog, k4, k2tog tbl, k14[20:26:30], k2tog, k4, k2tog tbl, k11[16:21:24]. 108[138:168:188] sts. Work 1 row straight as set. Cont to dec as set on last 4 rows at front edge on next row and foll 4th rows, and on armholes and sleeves on next row and foll alt rows, until 62[56:50:52] sts rem.

1st and 2nd sizes only:
Keeping front edges straight, cont to dec as before on armholes and sleeves on next 2[1] alt rows. 46[48] sts.

All sizes:
Work 1 row.
Next row: (RS) K2tog, k3, k2tog tbl, k2tog, k3, k2tog tbl, k18[20:22:24], k2tog, k3, k2tog tbl, k2tog, k3, k2tog tbl. 38[40:42:44] sts.
Next row: K9, p20[22:24:26], k9.
Next row: K2tog, k1, k2tog tbl, k2tog, k2, k2tog tbl, k16[18:20:22], k2tog, k2, k2tog tbl, k2tog, k1, k2tog tbl. 30[32:34:36] sts.
Work 1 row straight as set. Cast/bind off firmly.

COLLAR:
Left side: Sl 5 sts from left front safety-pin on to 10mm (no. 000/US 15) needles and with RS facing, join yarn at inside edge. ** K2 rows. Cont in g st, inc 1 st at inside edge on next and foll alt rows to 14[15:16:18] sts, then on foll 4th rows to 17[18:19:21] sts. K2 rows, ending at outside edge. Place marker at beg of last row.
Shape collar:
Next row: K10[10:11:11], turn.
Next row: Sl 1, k to end.
Next row: K9[9:10:10], k1 tbl, k to end. K3 rows. Rep last 6 rows 3 times more, ending at outside edge.
3rd and 4th sizes only:
K2 rows straight. **
All sizes:
Cut off yarn and leave sts on holder.
Right side: Sl 5 sts from right front safety-pin on to 10mm (no. 000/US 15) needles and with WS facing, join yarn at inside edge. Work as left side of collar from ** to **. Do not cut off yarn.
All sizes:
Sl sts from left collar on to spare needle with end of yarn at

needle point. Holding both needles in left hand, with points and WS tog, right front in front of left front, cast/bind off both pieces tog, taking 1 st from right front tog with 1 st from left front for each st.

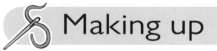 ## Making up

Sew collar to neck edge, placing markers in line with centre of raglans. Join side and sleeve seams. Sew on buttons.

Flower throw

Three-dimensional flowers add a quirky touch to this throw, which is easy and fun to knit.

The alternating blocks of plain stocking/stockinette stitch and striped garter stitch give this throw a woven effect. Three-dimensional 'frilly' flowers and leaves on several of the blocks add an attractive finishing touch.

GETTING STARTED

Each block is easy to work in either stocking/stockinette stitch or garter stitch. The flowers and leaves are also simple to make

Size:
Throw measures 100cm x 150cm (40in x 60in); each block is 25cm x 30cm (10in x 12in)

How much yarn:
11 x 50g (2oz) balls of Debbie Bliss Cashmerino Chunky, approx 65m (71 yards) per ball, in main colour A
8 balls in contrast colour B
6 balls in contrast colour C
1 ball in contrast colour D
1 ball in contrast colour E

Needles:
Pair of 5.5mm (no. 5/US 9) knitting needles

Additional items:
5mm (no. 6/US 8) crochet hook for edging

Tension/gauge:
14 sts and 20 rows measure 10cm (4in) square over st st on 5.5mm (no. 5/US 9) needles
IT IS ESSENTIAL TO WORK TO THE STATED TENSION/GAUGE TO ACHIEVE SUCCESS

What you have to do:
Work equal numbers of blocks in stocking/stockinette stitch and garter stitch. Stripe garter-stitch blocks in two colours, carrying yarns up side of work. Make separate flowers and leaves. Sew blocks together to form throw, then crochet edging all round. Sew on flowers to some stocking/stockinette stitch blocks.

The Yarn
Debbie Bliss Cashmerino Chunky is a luxurious blend of 55% merino wool, 33% microfibre and 12% cashmere. Its soft handle means that the finished fabric drapes well, which is perfect for a throw. There is a sophisticated colour range to choose from, with plenty of colours to coordinate with all your home furnishings.

Abbreviations:

alt = alternate;
beg = beginning;
ch = chain;
cm = centimetre(s);
cont = continue;
dc = double crochet (US
sc = single crochet);
foll = follows;
g st = garter stitch (every
row knit);
inc = increase;
k = knit; **p** = purl;
psso = pass slipped stitch
over; **rem** = remaining;
RS = right side; **sl** = slip;
st(s) = stitch(es);
st st = stocking/stockinette
stitch; **tog** = together;
yfwd = yarn forward/
yarn over

Instructions

BLOCK 1: (Make 10)

With A, cast on 35 sts. Beg with a k row, cont in st st until block measures 30cm (12in) from beg, ending with a p row. Cast/bind off.

BLOCK 2: (Make 10)

With B, cast on 35 sts. K2 rows. Join in C and k 2 rows. Cont in g st and
2 rows each of B and C until block measures 30cm (12in) from beg, ending with a WS row. Cast/bind off.

LEAVES: (Make 5)

With B, cast on 3 sts, leaving a long end to attach leaf to throw. Beg with a k row, work 4 rows in st st.
1st row: K1, (yfwd, k1) twice. 5 sts.
2nd and foll alt rows: P to end.
3rd row: K2, yfwd, k1, yfwd, k2. 7 sts.
5th row: K3, yfwd, k1, yfwd, k3. 9 sts.
7th row: K1, sl 1, k1, psso, k1, (yfwd, k1) twice, k2tog, k1. 9 sts.
8th row: P to end.
9th–12th rows: Rep 7th and 8th rows twice more.
13th row: K1, sl 1, k1, psso, k to last 3 sts, k2tog, k1. 7 sts.
14th row: P to end.
15th and 16th rows: As 13th and 14th rows. 5 sts.

17th row: K1, sl 1, k1, psso, k2tog.
18th row: P to end.
19th row: Sl 1, k1, psso, k1.
Cut off yarn and thread through rem 2 sts, draw up and fasten off.

FLOWERS:

(Make 5–3 as here and 2 more reversing colours)
With D, cast on 8 sts, leaving a long end. K3 rows. Cut off D and join in E.
Inc row: K1, *yfwd, k1, rep from * to last st, k1. 14 sts. K2 rows. Rep last 3 rows twice more, then work inc row again. 98 sts. Cast/bind off as foll:
Next row: *K2tog, sl st on right-hand needle back on to left-hand needle, rep from * to end, fasten off last st on right-hand needle.
Thread yarn end from cast-on into needle and working running sts along cast-on edge, draw up to gather. Join side seam, changing colour as appropriate.

HOW TO
CROCHET THE EDGING

The edges of the throw are bound with a single row of double crochet (US sc), each one worked in every third stitch or fourth row end and separated by three chain stitches.

1 With the right side of the throw facing, take the crochet hook through the fabric just below the cast/bound-off row or the last stitch of the row. Pick up a loop of yarn B with the hook and bring it back through to the right side of the work.

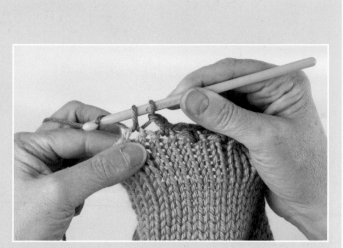

3 Miss two stitches and take the hook through to the back in the next stitch. Wrap the yarn around the hook and bring through to the front. Wrap the yarn around the hook once more and pull this loop through the two loops on the crochet hook to make a double crochet (US sc). Repeat steps 2 and 3 along edge of the throw.

2 Wrap the yarn over the hook at the back of the fabric and pull it through the loop at the front to make one chain. Repeat this twice more to give a total of three chains.

4 Work two double crochet (US sc) in each corner stitch to turn the corner and continue in this way around all edges of the throw.

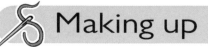 Making up

Pin out stocking/stockinette stitch blocks only to given measurements and lightly press using a warm iron over a dry cloth. Alternating blocks, join them together as shown in photograph (above left), with 5 rows consisting of 4 blocks in each row.

Edging: With crochet hook, B and RS of throw facing, start at one corner and work *3ch, miss 2 sts (or 3 row ends), 1dc (US sc) in next st (or row end) on throw, rep from * all round outer edges.

Attach flowers and leaves to centre of stocking/stockinette stitch blocks.

Cable scarf

Here is an easy pattern to practise your cabling skills and make an impressive scarf.

This stunning scarf is worked in a cosy, loosely spun yarn and a features an impressive cable pattern.

GETTING STARTED

No shaping required but you will need to practise working cables

Size:
Scarf is 19cm wide x 167cm long (7½in x 66in), excluding fringe

How much yarn:
5 x 100g (3½oz) balls of Rowan Cocoon, approx 115m (126 yards) per ball

Needles:
Pair of 7mm (no. 2/US 10½) knitting needles
Cable needle

Tension/gauge:
14 sts and 18 rows measure 10cm (4in) square over stocking/stockinette stitch on 7mm (no. 2/US 10½) needles
IT IS ESSENTIAL TO WORK TO THE STATED TENSION/GAUGE TO ACHIEVE SUCCESS

What you have to do:
Cast on loosely. Work throughout in cable pattern as directed. Cast/bind off in pattern. Knot a fringe along both short ends of scarf.

The Yarn
Rowan Cocoon contains 80% merino wool and 20% kid mohair. It is a loosely spun luxurious yarn that produces a soft and warm fabric. There is a good selection of muted contemporary colours to choose from.

Abbreviations:
beg = beginning; **cm** = centimetre(s); **cont** = continue; C6 = cable 6 sts as foll: sl next 3 sts on to cable needle and hold at front of work, k3, then k 3 sts from cable needle; **foll** = follows; **k** = knit; **patt** = pattern; **p** = purl; **rep** = repeat; **RS** = right side; **sl** = slip; **st(s)** = stitch(es)

Instructions

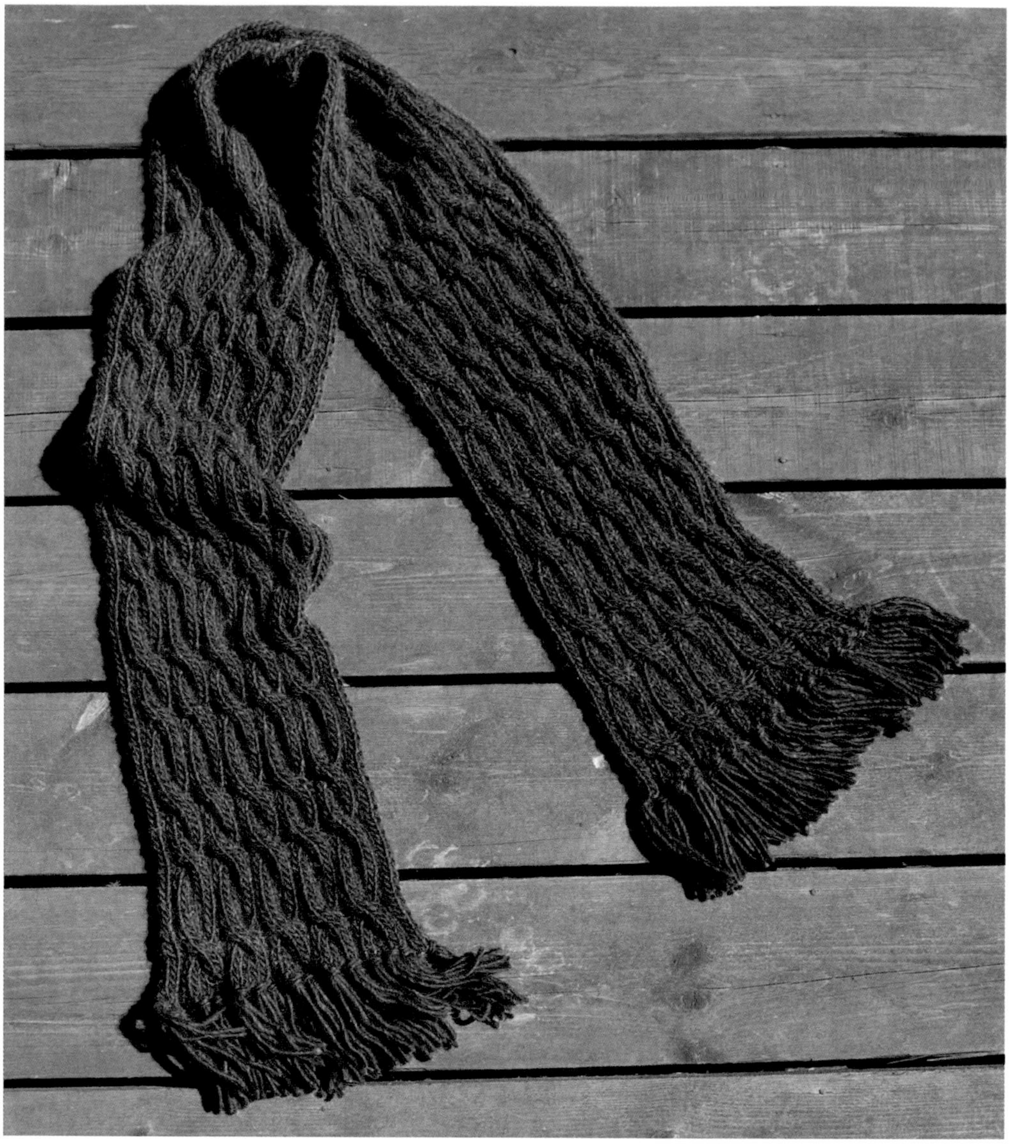

SCARF:
With 7mm (no. 2/US 10½) needles cast on 48 sts loosely. Cont in cable patt as foll:
1st row: (RS) K3, (p2, k6) 5 times, p2, k3.
2nd row: P3, (k2, p6) 5 times, k2, p3.
3rd–6th rows: Rep 1st and 2nd rows twice more.
7th row: K3, (p2, C6) 5 times, p2, k3.
8th row: As 2nd row.
9th–18th rows: Rep 1st and 2nd rows 5 times more.
19th row: As 7th row.
20th row: As 2nd row.
These 20 rows form patt. Rep them throughout until Scarf measures approximately 167cm (66in) from beg, ending with a 4th patt row. Cast/bind off evenly in patt.

Fringe:
Cut yarn into 25cm (10in) lengths. Taking two strands together each time, knot a tassel into alternate sts along both short ends of Scarf. Trim fringe to approximately 9cm (3½in) long.

Aran jacket with shawl collar

Combine traditional Aran patterns with contemporary styling to create a classic with a twist.

Worked in traditional Aran stitches, this button-through jacket with shawl collar is right up to date with its loose, coat-like construction.

GETTING STARTED

 This beautiful jacket is an exciting challenge for accomplished knitters

Size:

To fit bust: 81–91[97–107]cm/32½–36[38–42]in

Actual size: 97[117]cm/38[46]in

Length: 64[68]cm/25[26½]in

Sleeve seam: 46cm (18in)

Note: Figures in square brackets [ ] refer to larger size; where there is only one set of figures, it applies to both sizes

How much yarn:

7[9] x 100g (3½oz) balls of King Cole Fashion Aran, approx 200m (219 yards) per ball

Needles:

Pair of 4mm (no. 8/US 6) knitting needles

Pair of 5mm (no. 6/US 8) knitting needles

Cable needle

Additional items:

3 buttons, Stitch holders

Tension/gauge:

25 sts and 25 rows measure 10cm (4in) square over patt on 5mm (no. 6/US 8) needles

IT IS ESSENTIAL TO WORK TO THE STATED TENSION/GAUGE TO ACHIEVE SUCCESS

What you have to do:

Work throughout in cable pattern. Knit separate pocket linings and insert for set-in pockets on fronts. Work front band and collar in garter stitch, knitting in one with fronts. Make cast/bound-off buttonholes in right front band.

The Yarn

King Cole Fashion Aran combines the practicality of 70% acrylic with the good looks of 30% wool. It is available in an excellent range of natural-looking shades and you can even machine wash the finished garment.

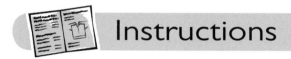 # Instructions

Abbreviations:

alt = alternate; **beg** = beginning; **cm** = centimetre(s); **cn** = cable needle; **cont** = continue; **foll** = follow(s)(ing); **g st** = garter stitch (k every row); **inc** = increase(ing); **k** = knit; **m l** = make one stitch by picking up strand lying between needles and working into back of it; **p** = purl; **patt** = pattern; **rep** = repeat; **rem** = remaining; **RS** = right side; **sl** = slip; **st(s)** = stitch(es); **st st** = stocking/stockinette stitch; **tbl** = through back of loop(s); **tog** = together; **WS** = wrong side;

C4B = sl next 2 sts on to cn and leave at back of work, k2, then k2 from cn

C4F = sl next 2 sts on to cn and leave at front of work, k2, then k2 from cn

BC = sl next st on to cn and leave at back of work, k2, then p1 from cn

FC = sl next 2 sts on to cn and leave at front of work, p1, then k2 from cn

LT = sl next st on to cn and leave at front of work, p1, then k1 tbl from cn

RT = sl next st on to cn and leave at back of work, k1 tbl, then p1 from cn

BACK:

With 4mm (no. 8/US 6) needles cast on 121[147] sts.

Next row: P to end. Change to 5mm (no. 6/US 8) needles. Work in patt as foll:

1st row: (RS) K2, *k1 tbl, p4, k3 tbl, p4, k1 tbl, p2, FC, BC, FC, p2, rep from * to last 15 sts, k1 tbl, p4, k3 tbl, p4, k1 tbl, k2.

2nd row: K2, *p1, k4, p3 tbl, k4, p1, k2, p2, k2, p4, k3, rep from * to last 15 sts, p1, k4, p3 tbl, k4, p1, k2.

3rd row: K2, *k1 tbl, p3, RT, k1 tbl, LT, p3, k1 tbl, p3, C4F, p2, k2, p2, rep from * to last 15 sts, k1 tbl, p3, RT, k1 tbl, LT, p3, k1 tbl, k2.

4th row: K2, *p1, k3, (p1 tbl, k1) twice, p1 tbl, k3, p1, k2, p2, k2, p4, k3, rep from * to last 15 sts, p1, k3, (p1 tbl, k1) twice, p1 tbl, k3, p1, k2.

5th row: K2, *k1 tbl, p2, RT, p1, k1 tbl, p1, LT, p2, k1 tbl, p2, BC, FC, BC, p2, rep from * to last 15 sts, k1 tbl, p2, RT, p1, k1 tbl, p1, LT, p2, k1 tbl, k2.

6th row: K2, *p1, k2, (p1 tbl, k2) twice, p1 tbl, k2, p1, k3, p4, k2, p2, k2, rep from * to last 15 sts, p1, k2, (p1 tbl, k2) twice, p1 tbl, k2, p1, k2.

7th row: K2, *k1 tbl, p1, RT, p1, k3 tbl, p1, LT, p1, k1 tbl, p2, k2, p2, C4B, p3, rep from * to last 15 sts, k1 tbl, p1, RT, p1, k3 tbl, p1, LT, p1, k1 tbl, k2.

8th row: K2, *p1, k1, p1 tbl, k2, p3 tbl, k2, p1 tbl, k1, p1, k3, p4, k2, p2, k2, rep from * to last 15 sts, p1, k1, p1 tbl, k2, p3 tbl, k2, p1 tbl, k1, p1, k2. These 8 rows form patt and

are repeated throughout. Cont in patt until work measures 43cm (17in) from beg, ending with a WS row.

Shape armholes:

Cast/bind off 13 sts at beg of next 2 rows. 95[121] sts. Cont in patt until armholes measure 21[25]cm/8¼[10]in from beg, ending with a WS row.

Shape shoulders:

Cast/bind off 7[10] sts at beg of next 6 rows and 8[10] sts at beg of foll 2 rows. Cast/bind off rem 37[41] sts.

POCKET LININGS: (Make 2)

With 5mm (no. 6/US 8) needles cast on 26 sts. Beg with a k row, work in st st to 13cm (5in), ending with a RS row.

Next row: P4, *m1, p2, rep from * 8 times more, m1, p4. 36 sts. Cut off yarn and leave sts on a holder.

LEFT FRONT:

With 4mm (no. 8/US 6) needles cast on 62[74] sts.

Next row: P to end.

Change to 5mm (no. 6/US 8) needles. Cont in patt as foll:

1st size only:

1st row: (RS) K2, *k1 tbl, p4, k3 tbl, p4, k1 tbl, p2, FC, BC, FC, p2, rep from * to last 8 sts, k1 tbl, k7.

2nd row: K7, p1, *k2, p2, k2, p4, k3, p1, k4, p3 tbl, k4, p1, rep from * to last 2 sts, k2.

2nd size only:

1st row: (RS) K2, *k1 tbl, p4, k3 tbl, p4, k1 tbl, p2, FC, BC, FC, p2, rep from * to last 20 sts, k1 tbl, p4, k3 tbl, p4, k1 tbl, k7.

2nd row: K7, *p1, k4, p3 tbl, k4, p1, k2, p2, k2, p4, k3, rep from * to last 15 sts, p1, k4, p3 tbl, k4, p1, k2.

Both sizes:

Cont as set, keeping 7 sts at front edge in g st for button band, until Front measures 16cm (6¼in) from beg, ending on WS.

Place pocket:

Next row: Patt 10[16] sts, sl next 36 sts onto a holder, patt across 36 sts from one pocket lining, patt to end.

Cont in patt until Front is 8 rows shorter than Back to armhole, ending with a WS row.

Shape collar and front edge:

1st row: Patt to last 10 sts, work 2tog, k1 tbl, m1, k7.

2nd and 4th rows: K8, p1, patt to end.

3rd row: Patt to last 9 sts, k1 tbl, k8.

5th row: Patt to last 11 sts, work 2tog, k1 tbl, m1, k8.

6th and 8th rows: K9, p1, patt to end.

7th row: Patt to last 10 sts, k1 tbl, k9.

Shape armhole:

9th row: Cast/bind off 13 sts, patt to last 12 sts, work 2tog, k1 tbl, m1, k9. 49[61] sts.

Keeping armhole edge straight, cont as foll:

10th and 12th rows: K10, p1, patt to end.

11th row: Patt to last 11 sts, k1 tbl, k10.

13th row: Patt to last 13 sts, work 2tog, k1 tbl, m1, k10.

Cont to shape collar and front edge as now set on every foll 4th row until the row 'Patt to last 21[19] sts, work 2tog, k1 tbl, m1, k18[16]' has been worked, then on every foll 6th row until the row 'Patt to last 22[23] sts, work 2tog, k1 tbl, m1, k19[20]' has been worked.

Work straight until armhole measures same as Back to beg of shoulder shaping, ending with a WS row.

Shape shoulder:

Cast/bind off 7[10] sts at beg of next and foll 2 alt rows, then 8[10] sts at beg of next alt row.

Cut off yarn and leave rem 20[21] sts on a holder for Collar.

Mark the positions of 3 buttons on button band, the first 20cm (8in) up from cast-on edge, the last 2cm (¾in) down from start of collar with the remaining one spaced evenly between.

RIGHT FRONT:

With 4mm (no. 8/US 6) needles cast on 62[74] sts.

Next row: P to end.

Change to 5mm (no. 6/US 8) needles. Work in patt as foll:

1st size only:

1st row: (RS) K7, k1 tbl, *p2, FC, BC, FC, p2, k1 tbl, p4, k3

tbl, p4, k1 tbl, rep from * to last 2 sts, k2.

2nd row: K2, *p1, k4, p3 tbl, k4, p1, k2, p2, k2, p4, k3, rep from * to last 8 sts, p1, k7.

2nd size only:

1st row: (RS) K7, *k1 tbl, p4, k3 tbl, p4, k1 tbl, p2, FC, BC, FC, p2, rep from * to last 15 sts, k1 tbl, p4, k3 tbl, p4, k1 tbl, k2.

2nd row: K2, *p1, k4, p3 tbl, k4, p1, k2, p2, k2, p4, k3, rep from * to last 20 sts, p1, k4, p3 tbl, k4, p1, k7.

Both sizes:

Work as now set, keeping 7 sts at front edge in g st for buttonhole band, until Front measures 16cm (6¼in) from beg, ending with a WS row.

Place pocket:

Next row: K7, patt 9[15] sts, sl next 36 sts onto a holder, patt across 36 sts from other pocket lining, patt to end.

Cont in patt making buttonholes to correspond with markers on Left front as foll:

1st buttonhole row: (RS) K3, cast/bind off next 2 sts, patt to end.

2nd buttonhole row: Patt to end, casting on 2 sts over those cast/bound off on previous row.

Cont in patt until Front is 8 rows shorter than Back to armhole, ending with a WS row.

Shape collar and front edge:

1st row: K7, m1, k1 tbl, work 2tog, patt to end.

2nd and 4th rows: Patt to last 9 sts, p1, k8.

3rd row: K8, k1 tbl, patt to end.

5th row: K8, m1, k1 tbl, work 2tog, patt to end.

6th row: Patt to last 10 sts, p1, k9.

7th row: K9, k1 tbl, patt to end.

Shape armhole:

8th row: Cast/bind off 13 sts, patt to last 10 sts, p1, k9.

Keep armhole edge straight, cont as foll:

9th row: K9, m1, k1 tbl, work 2tog, patt to end.

Cont to shape collar and front edge as now set on every foll 4th row until the row 'K18[16], m1, k1 tbl, work 2tog, patt to end' has been worked, then on every foll 6th row until the row 'K19[20], m1, k1 tbl, work 2tog, patt to end' has been worked. Cont straight until armhole measures same as Back to beg of shoulder shaping, ending with a RS row.

Shape shoulder:

Cast/bind off 7[10] sts at beg of next and foll 2 alt rows and 8 [10] sts at beg of next row.

Cut off yarn and leave rem 20[21] sts on a holder for Collar.

SLEEVES:

With 4mm (no. 8/US 6) needles cast on 69[75] sts.

Next row: P to end.

Change to 5mm (no. 6/US 8) needles. Cont in patt as foll:

1st size only:

Work as given for Back. Work 3 rows.

2nd size only:

1st row: (RS) P4, k1 tbl, *p2, FC, BC, FC, p2, k1 tbl, p4, k3 tbl, p4, k1 tbl, rep from * to last 18 sts, p2, FC, BC, FC, p2, k1 tbl, p4.

2nd row: K4, p1, *k2, p2, k2, p4, k3, p1, k4, p3 tbl, k4, p1, rep from * to last 18 sts, k2, p2, k2, p4, k3, p1, k4.

3rd row: K1 tbl, p3, k1 tbl, *p3, C4F, p2, k2, p2, k1 tbl, p3, RT, k1 tbl, LT, p3, k1 tbl, rep from * to last 18 sts, p3, C4F, p2, k2, p2, k1 tbl, p3, k1 tbl.

Both sizes:

Work in patt as now set, AT SAME TIME inc 1 st at each end of next and every foll 4th row to 77[123] sts, then on every foll 6th row to 105[125] sts, working increased sts into patt. Work straight until Sleeve measures 46cm (18in) from beg, ending with a WS row. Insert a marker at each end of last row. Cont straight for a further 5cm (2in), ending with a WS row.

Shape top:

Cast/bind off 21[25] sts at beg of next 4 rows. Cast/bind off rem 21[25] sts.

POCKET TOPS:

With 4mm (no. 8/US 6) needles and RS of work facing, rejoin yarn to sts on holder and work as foll:

Next row: K3, *k2tog, k1, rep from * 8 times more, k2tog, k4. 26 sts. K 3 more rows. Cast/bind off.

BACK COLLAR: (Work both sides alike)

With 5mm (no. 6/US 8) needles and RS of work facing, rejoin yarn to inside edge of Collar. Work in g st until Collar fits to centre of back neck. Cast/bind off.

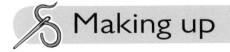 # Making up

Sew shoulder seams. Join cast/bound-off edges of collar, then sew to back neck. With centre of sleeve tops to shoulder seams, sew in sleeves, sewing row ends above markers to cast/bound-off sts at underarms. Join side and sleeve seams. Slip stitch pocket linings in place on WS, and ends of pocket tops on RS, of fronts. Sew on buttons.

Fruity fun egg cosies

Brighten up your breakfast table with this set of fruit-themed egg cosies.

Keep boiled eggs warm with these fruity cosies. The strawberry, apple and pineapple cosies are based on stocking/stockinette stitch with added decorative details, while the blackberry cosy is in a crunchy textured stitch.

GETTING STARTED

Set involves some interesting techniques that are easy to try out on small pieces

Size:
Each cosy is approximately 7cm high x 15cm in diameter (2¾in x 6in)

How much yarn:
1 x 50g (2oz) ball of Patons Diploma Gold DK, approx 120m (131 yards) per ball, in each of eight colours A – red, B – white, C – lemon, D – apple green, E – plum, F – dark green, G – honey and H – ginger

Needles:
Pair of 4mm (no. 8/US 6) knitting needles

Additional items:
3.5mm (no. 9/US 4/E) crochet hook

Tension/gauge:
22 sts and 28 rows measure 10cm (4in) square over st st on 4mm (no. 8/US 6) needles
IT IS ESSENTIAL TO WORK TO THE STATED TENSION/ GAUGE TO ACHIEVE SUCCESS

What you have to do:
Work single (knit one, purl one) rib at lower edge of all cosies. Work strawberry cosy in stocking/stockinette stitch with knitted-in 'pips' in a second colour. Work blackberry cosy in textured stitch pattern. Work apple cosy in stocking/stockinette stitch with embroidered motif on front. Work pineapple cosy in stocking/ stockinette stitch with coloured diamond pattern using intarsia techniques. Make knitted leaves and crochet loops and motifs for tops of cosies.

The Yarn
Patons Diploma Gold DK is a practical mixture of 55% wool, 25% acrylic and 20% nylon. It is ideal for items that will need cleaning as it can be machine washed.
There is a good palette with plenty of choice for this colourful set.

 Instructions

Abbreviations:
alt = alternate; **beg** = beginning; **ch** = chain; **cm** = centimetre(s); **cont** = continue; **dc** = double crochet (US **sc** = single crochet); **dec** = decreasing; **foll** = follow(s)(ing); **inc** = increasing; **k** = knit; **p** = purl; **patt** = pattern; **rem** = remaining; **rep** = repeat; **RS** = right side; **ss** = slipstitch (crochet); **st(s)** = stitch(es); **st st** = stocking/stockinette stitch; **tog** = together; **WS** = wrong side

STRAWBERRY COSY:

With A, cast on 31 sts.

1st row: (RS) K1, *p1, k1, rep from * to end.

2nd row: P1, *k1, p1, rep from * to end.

3rd row: As 1st row.

P 1 row. Join in B and cont in st st and spot patt as foll, stranding yarn not in use loosely across WS of work.

1st row: (RS) K3 A, *1 B, 3 A, rep from * to end.

2nd row: With A, p to end.

3rd row: With A, k to end.

4th row: P1 A, 1 B, *3 A, 1 B, rep from * to last st, 1 A.

5th row: With A, k to end.

6th row: With A, p to end. Rep these 6 rows once more. Cut off B and cont in A only.

Next row: K to end.

Next row: P2, *p2tog, p3, rep from * to last 4 sts, p2tog, p2. 25 sts.

Next row: K to end.

Next row: P2, *p2tog, p2, rep from * to last 3 sts, p2tog, p1. 19 sts.

Next row: K to end.

Cut off yarn, leaving a long end for sewing seam. Thread cut end through rem sts, draw up tightly and fasten off.

Leaf:

With D, cast on 7 sts. Beg with a k row, cont in st st and work 4 rows. Dec 1 st at each end of next and foll alt row. 3 sts.

Next row: P3tog and fasten off.

Flowers: (Make 2)

With crochet hook and C, make 4ch. Join with a ss into first ch to form a ring. Make petals by working (4ch, 1dc (US sc) into ring) 5 times, 8ch. Fasten off.

BLACKBERRY COSY:

With E, cast on 31 sts.

1st row: (RS) K1, *p1, k1, rep from * to end.

2nd row: P1, *k1, p1, rep from * to end.

3rd row: As 1st row. Cont in patt as foll:

1st row: (WS) K2, *(k1, p1, k1) all into next st, p3tog, rep from * to last st, k1.

2nd row: P to end.

3rd row: K2, *p3tog, (k1, p1, k1) all into next st, rep from * to last st, k1.

4th row: P to end. Rep these 4 rows twice more, then work 1st and 2nd rows again.

Next row: (WS) K2, *p3tog, p1, rep from * to last st, k1. 17 sts.

Cut off yarn, leaving a long end for sewing seam. Thread cut end through rem sts, draw up tightly and fasten off.

APPLE COSY:

With D, cast on 31 sts.

1st row: (RS) K1, *p1, k1, rep from * to end.

2nd row: P1, *k1, p1, rep from * to end.

3rd row: As 1st row.

P 1 row, inc 1 st at each end and centre of row. 34 sts. Beg with a k row, work 8 rows in st st.

Next row: (RS) K4, k2tog, *k6, k2tog, rep from * to last 4 sts, k4. 30 sts.

Next row: P to end.

Next row: (RS) K3, k2tog, *k5, k2tog, rep from * to last 4 sts, k4. 26 sts.

Next row: P to end.

Next row: (RS) K2, k2tog, *k4, k2tog, rep from * to last 4 sts, k4. 22 sts.

Next row: P to end.

Next row: (RS) K1, k2tog, *k3, k2tog, rep from * to last 4 sts, k4. 18 sts.

Next row: P to end.

Next row: *K2tog, rep from * to end. 9 sts.

Cut off yarn, leaving a long end for sewing seam. Thread cut end through rem sts, draw up tightly and fasten off.

Leaves:

With F, make two leaves as given for Strawberry cosy.

PINEAPPLE COSY:

With G, cast on 31 sts.

1st row: (RS) K1, *p1, k1, rep from * to end.
2nd row: P1, *k1, p1, rep from * to end.
3rd row: As 1st row.

Beg with a p row, cont in st st and patt from chart, working odd-numbered (WS) rows from left to right and even-numbered (RS) rows from right to left. Strand colour not in use loosely across WS of work. Cont in patt from chart until 15 rows have been completed.

Next row: (RS) With H, k2tog, *k1 H, 1 C, 1 H, with H, k3tog, rep from * to last 5 sts, k1 H, 1 C, 1 H, with H, k2tog. 21 sts.
Next row: *P1 H, 3 C, rep from * to last st, 1 H.
Next row: With C, *k1, k2tog, rep from * to end. 14 sts.

Cut off yarn, leaving a long end for sewing seam. Thread cut end through rem sts, draw up tightly and fasten off.

Leaves:

Make three leaves as given for Strawberry cosy – two in F and one in D.

BLACKBERRY COSY:

Join back seam. With crochet hook and F, make 15ch. Form into a loop and sew securely to top of cosy.

APPLE COSY:

Join back seam. With C, work 5 diagonal straight sts, about 1cm (½in) long, in centre of front. Working under and over each strand, weave another 5 straight sts through first set, working in opposite direction. Sew leaves securely to top of cosy. With crochet hook and H, make 15ch. Fasten off. Form into a loop and sew securely to top of cosy in centre of leaves.

PINEAPPLE COSY:

Join back seam. Sew leaves securely to top of cosy. With crochet hook and D, make 15ch. Fasten off. Form into a loop and sew securely to top of cosy in centre of leaves.

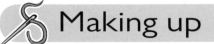
Making up

STRAWBERRY COSY:

Join back seam. Sew in starting end on flowers and sew ch end to top of cosy, make a small pleat in cast-on edge of leaf and sew to top of cosy. With crochet hook and D, make 15ch. Fasten off. Form into a loop and sew securely next to leaf on top of cosy.

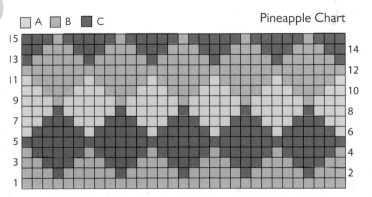
Pineapple Chart
☐ A ▨ B ▦ C

Funky bobble hat

Perfect for the ski slopes or a walk in the countryside, this bobble hat is quick and easy to make.

Spot-on for winter, this trendy hat with its giant pompom is decorated with felt circles that are stitched on afterwards.

GETTING STARTED

Quick and easy to make in chunky yarn and basic fabric

Size:

To fit an average woman's head

Actual size around brim: *55cm (21½in)*

How much yarn:

1 x 100g ball of Sirdar Denim Chunky, approx 156m (171 yards) per ball

Needles:

Pair of 5.5mm (no. 5/US 9) knitting needles

Pair of 6.5mm (no. 3/US 10½) knitting needles

Additional items:

Felt for circles

Sewing needle and thread

Tension/gauge:

14 sts and 19 rows measure 10cm (4in) square over st st on 6.5mm (no. 3/US 10½) needles

IT IS ESSENTIAL TO WORK TO THE STATED TENSION/GAUGE TO ACHIEVE SUCCESS

What you have to do:

Work in single (k1, p1) rib for brim. Work in stocking/stockinette stitch for main fabric. Decrease to shape crown. Sew on felt circles to decorate. Make a pompom.

The Yarn

Sirdar Denim Chunky is a practical mixture of 60% acrylic, 25% cotton and 15% wool that can be machine washed. There is a colour palette of chalky denim blues and mainly natural shades that are ideal for casual wear.

 ## Instructions

Abbreviations:

alt = alternate; **beg** = beginning; **cm** = centimetre(s); **cont** = continue; **foll** = follows; **k** = knit;   **p** = purl; **rem** = remaining; **rep** = repeat; **RS** = right side; **st(s)** = stitch(es); **st st** = stocking/stockinette stitch; **tog** = together; **WS** = wrong side

HAT:

With 5.5mm (no. 5/US 9) needles cast on 77 sts.

1st row: (RS) K1, *p1, k1, rep from * to end.

2nd row: P1, *k1, p1, rep from * to end.

Rep these 2 rows to form rib for 12cm (4¾in), ending with a 1st row.

Change to 6.5mm (no. 3/US 10½) needles.

Beg with a k row, cont in st st until work measures 22cm (8¾in) from beg, ending with a WS row.

Shape crown:

1st row: K2, k2tog, *k5, k2tog, rep from * to last 3 sts, k3. 66 sts.

2nd and foll alt rows: P to end.

3rd row: K2, k2tog, *k4, k2tog, rep from * to last 2 sts, k2. 55 sts.

5th row: K1, k2tog, *k3, k2tog, rep from * to last 2 sts, k2. 44 sts.

7th row: K1, k2tog, *k2, k2tog, rep from * to last st, k1. 33 sts.

9th row: K2tog, *k1, k2tog, rep from * to last st, k1. 22 sts.

11th row: *K2tog, rep from * to end. 11 sts.

Cut off yarn, leaving a long end. Thread cut end through rem sts, draw up tightly and fasten off.

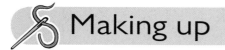 # Making up

Use long end of yarn to join back seam, reversing seam on brim.

Cut ten 4cm (1½in) diameter circles from felt. Position circles randomly around hat and, using contrasting coloured thread, sew in place.

Make a pompom approximately 14cm (5½in) in diameter and attach to top of hat. Turn back brim.

HOW TO
MAKE A POMPOM

Use this technique to make the large pompom for the top of the hat.

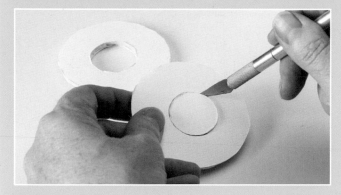

1 This pompom is 14cm (5½in) in diameter. Cut two circles of thick card that are slightly larger than the diameter of the finished pompom. Cut a circle from the centre of each disc.

2 Thread a large-eyed sewing needle with as many ends of yarn as you can fit through the eye. Each length of yarn should be approximately 1m (1 yard) long.

3 Hold the two discs one on top of the other. Thread the needle through the centre and hold the ends of the yarn with one thumb. Take the needle around the discs and back through the centre. Continue to do this, working your way evenly around the discs until the centre hole is full.

4 Using small sharp scissors, cut around the outside edge of the discs, snipping through all the layers of yarn.

5 Gently ease the discs apart so that there is a straight section of yarn visible between them. Take a short length of yarn and tie it firmly around the middle of the pompom, knotting it as tightly as possible.

6 Ease the discs off the pompom and fluff it up into a round shape. Trim around the pompom, turning it as you work, to give an even shape.

Man's Fair Isle slipover

Step back in time with this classic design knitted in traditional colours and Shetland yarn.

Traditional yarn, colours and bands of Fair Isle patterns will make this slipover a perennial favourite in his wardrobe.

The Yarn

Jamieson & Smith 2-ply Jumper Weight Shetland Wool is 100% pure Shetland wool that is equivalent to 4-ply hand knitting (fingering) yarn. It is used in the knitting of unique Fair Isle garments and there are masses of authentic colours and shades to choose from.

GETTING STARTED

Working Fair Isle patterns in several colours and shaping at same time requires skill and concentration

Size:

To fit chest: 91–97[102–107:112–117]cm/36–38[40–42:44–46]in

Actual size: 106[114:122]cm/42[45:48]in

Length: 63[65:67]cm/25[25½in:26]in

Note: Figures in square brackets [ ] refer to larger sizes; where there is only one set of figures, it applies to all sizes

How much yarn:

7[7:8] x 25g balls of Jamieson & Smith 2-ply Jumper Weight Shetland Wool, approx 115m (125 yards) per ball, in colour A

2[2:3] balls in colour B

2[2:2] balls in colour C

2[2:2] balls in colour D

2[2:2] balls in colour E

1[2:2] balls in colour F

Needles:

Pair of 2.75mm (no. 12/US 1) knitting needles

Pair of 3.25mm (no. 10/US 3) knitting needles

Additional items:

Stitch holder, marker and safety pin

Tension/gauge:

30 sts and 32 rows measure 10cm (4in) square over patt on 3.25mm (no. 10/US 3) needles

IT IS ESSENTIAL TO WORK TO THE STATED TENSION/GAUGE TO ACHIEVE SUCCESS

What you have to do:

Work welt in single (knit one, purl one) rib. Work main fabric in stocking/stockinette stitch. Read chart to work. Fair Isle pattern, joining in and cutting off colours as required. Strand yarn not in use across wrong side of work. Use simple shaping for armholes and neck. Pick up stitches around neck and armholes and work edgings in rib.

Instructions

Abbreviations:

alt = alternate; **beg** = beginning; **cm** = centimetre(s); **cont** = continue; **dec** = decrease(ing); **foll** = follow(s) (ing); **inc** = increase(ing); **k** = knit; **p** = purl; **patt** = pattern; **rem** = remain(ing); **rep** = repeat; **RS** = right side; **sl** = slip; **st(s)** = stitch(es); **st st** = stocking/stockinette stitch; **tbl** = through back of loops; **tog** = together; **WS** = wrong side

BACK:

With 2.75mm (no. 12/US 1) needles and A, cast on 137[147:157] sts.

1st row: (RS) K1, (p1, k1) to end.

2nd row: P1, (k1, p1) to end.

Rep these 2 rows 13 times more.

Change to 3.25mm (no. 10/US 3) needles.

Inc row: (RS) K5[4:3], (inc in next st, k5) to last 6[5:4] sts, inc in next st, k5[4:3]. 159[171:183] sts.

P 1 row. Beg with a k row, cont in st st, stranding yarns not in use loosely across WS of work and working from chart as foll:

1st row: (RS) Reading chart from right to left, k1, rep 12 sts of motif to last 2 sts, k2.

2nd row: Reading chart from left to right, p2, rep 12 sts of motif to last st, p1.

Cont in this way until 80 rows from chart have been completed.*

Patt 1st–26th[30th:34th] rows again, ending with a WS row.

Shape armholes:

Keeping patt correct, cast/bind off 6[7:8] sts at beg of next 2 rows. 147[157:167] sts. Dec 1 st at each end of next and every foll alt row until 127[135:143] sts rem. Patt 53 rows straight, ending after 20th[26th:32nd] patt row.

Shape shoulders:

Working in A[patt:A], cast/bind off 38[41:44] sts, work until there are 51[53:55] sts on right-hand needle, cast/bind off rem 38[41:44] sts. Cut off yarn and sl centre 51[53:55] sts on to a holder.

FRONT:

Work as given for Back to *. Patt 1st–22nd[26th:30th] rows again, ending with a WS row.

Divide for neck:

Next row: (RS) Patt 77[83:89] sts, k2tog, turn and

complete this side of neck first.

Next row: Patt to end.

Next row: Patt to last 2 sts, k2tog.

Next row: Patt to end.

Shape armhole:

Next row: Cast/bind off 6[7:8] sts, patt to last 2 sts, k2tog. 70[75:80] sts.

Keeping patt correct, dec 1 st at each end of every foll alt row until 50[53:56] sts rem. Keeping armhole edge straight, cont to dec 1 st at neck edge only on every foll 4th row until 38[41:44] sts rem. Patt 5 rows straight, ending after 20th[26th:32nd] patt row. Cast/bind off in A[patt:A].

With RS of work facing, sl centre st on to a safety-pin, rejoin yarn to rem 79[85:89] sts, k2tog, patt to end.

Next row: Patt to end.

Next row: K2tog, patt to end.

Rep last 2 rows once more.

Shape armhole:

Next row: Cast/bind off 6[7:8] sts, patt to end. 70[75:80] sts.

Complete to match first side, reversing shaping.

NECKBAND:

Join right shoulder seam.

With 2.75mm (no. 12/US 1) needles, A and RS of work

facing, pick up and k 78[80:82] sts down left front neck, k centre st (and mark this st), pick up and k 78[80:82] sts up right front neck and k across 51[53:55] back neck sts on holder. 208[214:220] sts.

1st row: (WS) K1, (p1, k1) to within 2 sts of centre st, k2tog, p1, k2tog tbl, (k1, p1) to end.

2nd row: K1, (p1, k1) to within 2 sts of centre st, p2tog tbl, k1, p2tog, (k1, p1) to end.

Cont in rib as set, dec 1 st at either side of centre st on every row, work 7 more rows. 190[196:202] sts. Cast/bind off in rib, dec as before.

ARMHOLE EDGINGS:

Join left shoulder and neckband seam.

With 2.75mm (no. 12/US 1) needles, A and RS of work facing, pick up and k 114[120:126] sts evenly around armhole edge. Work 9 rows in k1, p1 rib. Cast/bind off loosely in rib.

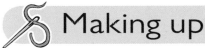 Making up

Block the garment by pinning out to correct size on a padded surface and spraying with clean, cold water. Smooth out and leave it to dry naturally. Join side and armhole edging seams.

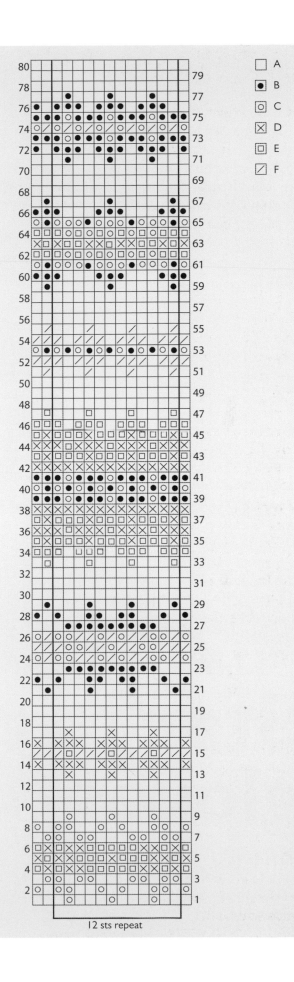

12 sts repeat

A
B
C
D
E
F

Star pattern gloves

Keep your hands cosy in these traditional gloves with a challenging pattern to knit.

With deep ribbed cuffs, an intarsia star pattern on the back of the hand and a diamond grid pattern on the palms, these gloves have been given a contemporary twist by working them in striking apple green and black.

The Yarn
Patons Diploma Gold DK is a mixture of 55% wool, 25% acrylic and 20% nylon, combining the good looks of wool with the practicality of man-made fibres. This is ideal for gloves as they can be machine washed. There is a good colour range to choose from for intarsia patterns.

GETTING STARTED

Working gloves in the round is quite skilful especially when there is an intarsia pattern to follow as well

Size:
To fit medium-size adult hands
Actual size around hand: 21.5cm (8½in)
Length of palm: 11cm (4¼in)

How much yarn:
2 x 50g (2oz) balls of Patons Diploma Gold DK in main colour A, approx 120m (131 yards) per ball
1 ball in contrast colour B

Needles:
Set of 3mm (no. 11/US 2) double-pointed needles

Set of 3.75mm (no. 9/US 5) double-pointed needles
Additional items:
Safety pins or stitch holders
Tension/gauge:
26 sts and 35 rows measure 10cm (4in) square over st st on 3mm (no. 11/US 2) needles
IT IS ESSENTIAL TO WORK TO STATED TENSION/GAUGE TO ACHIEVE SUCCESS

What you have to do:
Work in rounds on sets of four double-pointed needles. Work star pattern in two colours following charts. Strand colour not in use across wrong side of work. Leave sts on holders and complete thumb and fingers individually.

Abbreviations:
cm = centimetre(s);

cont = continue;

dec = decrease;

foll = follows; **k** = knit;

m1 = make one stitch: pick
up horizontal strand lying
between needles and knit
into back of it; **p** = purl;

patt = pattern;

p(2)sso = pass slipped
stitch(es) over;

RS = right side;

sl = slip;

st(s) = stitch(es);

st st = stocking/
stockinette stitch;

tog = together

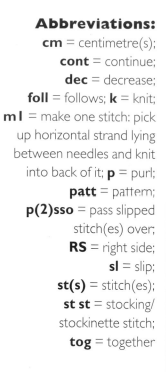 # Instructions

LEFT GLOVE:

With 3mm (no. 11/US 2) needles and A, cast on 16 sts on each of first 2 needles and 20 sts on 3rd needle. 52 sts.
To join in a round, bring yarn to front, sl first st on to 3rd needle, take yarn back between sts, sl first st back on to 1st needle and turn.

1st round: (RS) (K2, p2) to end.
This round forms rib. Rib 20 more rounds. K1 round.
Change to 3.75mm (no. 9) needles.

1st round: (RS) K (1 A, 1 B) to end.

2nd round: K (1 B, 1 A) to end. Change to 3mm (no. 11/US 2) needles. K2 rounds A **. Change to 3.75mm (no. 9/US 5) needles. Work in patt from charts as foll:

1st round: With A, m1, patt 25 sts of 1st row of Chart 1, with A, m1 and mark this st for the thumb gusset (1st row of Chart 3), patt 27 sts of 1st row of Chart 2. 54 sts.
This round sets position of charts for palm, thumb and back patterns. Cont in patt from charts, starting at right-hand edge of charts on every round and working m1 at each side of thumb gusset as indicated until 15 rounds have been

completed. 62 sts.

16th round: K1 A, patt 25 sts of 16th row of Chart 1, sl next 9 sts of thumb gusset on to a holder, with A cast on 4 sts, patt 27 sts of 16th row of Chart 2. 57 sts.
*** Cont in patt, working cast-on sts k4 A on every round, until 19th row of Charts 1 and 2 have been completed.
Change to 3mm (no. 11/US 2) needles. K2 rounds A.
Change to 3.75mm (no. 9/US 5) needles.

22nd round: With A, k2tog, k (1 B, 1 A) to last st, k1 B. 56 sts.

23rd round: K (1 B, 1 A) to end. Change to 3mm (no. 11/US 2) needles. Cont in A, k 4 rounds.

Divide for fingers:

Little finger: With 1st needle, k6, with 2nd needle, cast on 3 sts, leave next 44 sts of round on a holder, with 2nd needle, k next st, with 3rd needle, k last 5 sts. 15 sts. K 20 rounds.

Dec round: (Sl 2, k1, p2sso) 5 times. 5 sts.
Cut off yarn, leaving a long end. Thread end through sts, draw up and secure.

Ring finger: With 1st needle, k first 7 sts from holder, leave next 30 sts on holder and sl last 7 sts on to a spare needle, with 2nd needle, cast on 3 sts, k4 from spare needle, with 3rd needle, k3 from spare needle, k up 4 sts from base of 3 sts cast on for previous finger. 21 sts. K 1 round.

2nd round: K7, sl 2, k1, p2sso, k8, sl 2, k1, p2sso. 17 sts. K 24 rounds.

Dec round: K2tog, (sl 2, k1, p2sso) 5 times. 6 sts. Fasten off as little finger.

Middle finger: With 1st needle, leaving centre 16 sts on holder, work as given for ring finger but completing 26 rounds before working dec round.

Forefinger: With 1st needle, k6 from holder, with 2nd needle, k next 6 sts from holder, with 3rd needle, k last 4 sts from holder, k up 3 sts from cast-on sts of middle finger. 19 sts. K 1 round.

2nd round: K16, sl 2, k1, p2sso. 17 sts. Complete as ring finger.

Thumb: With 1st needle, k9 from holder, with 2nd needle, k up 3 sts from row ends and 2 sts from first 2 cast-on sts, with 3rd needle, k up 2 sts from next 2 cast-on sts and 3 sts from row ends. 19 sts. K18 rounds.

Dec round: (Sl 2, k1, p2sso) 6 times, k1. 7 sts. Fasten off as little finger.

RIGHT GLOVE:

Work as given for Left glove to **. Change to 3.75mm (no. 9/US 5) needles. Work in patt from charts as foll:

1st round: Patt 27 sts as 1st row of Chart 2, with A, m1 and mark this st for the thumb gusset (1st row of Chart 3), patt 25 sts of 1st row of Chart 1, with A, m1. 54 sts. This round sets position of charts for back, thumb and palm patterns. Cont in patt from charts working m1 at each side of thumb gusset as indicated until 15 rounds have been completed. 62 sts.

16th round: Patt 27 sts of 16th row of Chart 2, sl next 9 sts of thumb gusset on to a holder, with A cast on 4 sts, patt 25 sts of 16th row of Chart 1, k1 A. 57 sts. Complete as given for Left glove from *** to end.

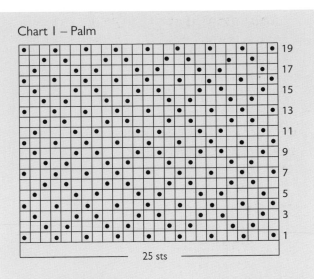

Chart 1 – Palm

25 sts

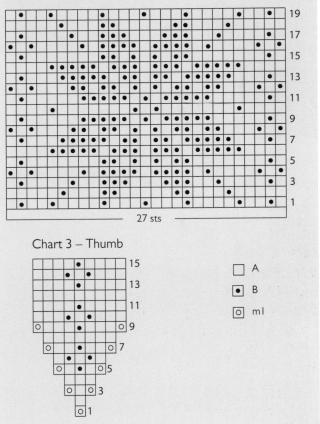

Chart 2 – Back of hand

27 sts

Chart 3 – Thumb

☐ A

◉ B

⊙ m1

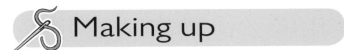

Making up

Turn inside out and press lightly. Darn in ends.

Sweetheart quilt

This quilt is easy to knit, while the colours and added embellishments make it a delightful addition to any bedroom.

Make a series of squares in soft ice-cream colours, then decorate with simple embroidery and sew together for a gorgeous quilt that will look stunning on a child's cot or bed.

GETTING STARTED

Worked in simple garter-stitch, squares are so easy to pick up and put down. Assemble finished quilt at your leisure

Size:
Quilt measures 80cm x 110cm (31½in x 43in)

How much yarn:
7 x 50g (2oz) balls of Debbie Bliss Cashmerino Aran, approx 90m (98 yards) per ball, in each of colours A and B
6 balls in colour C
5 balls in colour D
1 ball in each of colours E and F

Needles:
Pair of 5mm (no. 6/US 8) knitting needles

Additional items:
3.5mm (no. 9/US 4/E) crochet hook

Tension/gauge:
18 sts and 32 rows measure 10cm (4in) square over g st on 5mm (no. 6/US 8) needles
IT IS ESSENTIAL TO WORK TO THE STATED TENSION/GAUGE TO ACHIEVE SUCCESS

What you have to do:
Knit squares in plain garter stitch and embroider with chain-stitch heart. Knit squares in simple striped garter stitch. Knit squares in garter stitch with four stocking/stockinette stitch panels and Swiss darn heart motifs in these panels. Knit squares in garter stitch with central panel in stocking/stockinette stitch and Swiss darn heart motif in this panel. Crochet a simple edging around quilt.

The Yarn
Debbie Bliss Cashmerino Aran is a luxuriously soft mixture of 55% merino wool, 33% microfibre and 12% cashmere. The Aran (fisherman) weight makes it warm and cosy for a bed cover and quick to knit. There are plenty of colours to choose from so you can make up your own colour combinations to match your child's room.

Abbreviations:
cm = centimetre(s);
g st = garter stitch (every row knit);
k = knit; **p** = purl;
rep = repeat;
RS = right side;
st(s) = stitch(es);
st st = stocking/ stockinette stitch

SQUARE A: (Make 6)
With C, cast on 37 sts. Work in g st and stripe sequence of 10 rows each of C, D, E, A, B and F (60 rows in all). Cast/ bind off.

SQUARE B: (Make 6))
With B, cast on 37 sts. Work 60 rows in g st. Cast/bind off. Using template (opposite) as a guide, embroider the outline of a heart in chain stitch on each square using E.

SQUARE C: (Make 6)
With A, cast on 37 sts. Work 11 rows in g st.
Next row: K5, p11, k5, p11, k5.
Next row: K to end.
Rep last 2 rows 6 times more. Work 10 rows in g st.
Next row: K5, p11, k5, p11, k5.
Next row: K to end.

Rep last 2 rows 6 times more, then work first of them again. Work 10 rows in g st. Cast/bind off. Following the chart, Swiss darn a small heart motif in centre of each st st panel. Use E for bottom left panel, C for bottom right panel, F for top left panel and B for top right panel.

SQUARE D: (Make 3)
With D, cast on 37 sts.
Work 23 rows in g st.
Next row: K13, p11, k13.
Next row: K to end.
Rep the last 2 rows 7 times more. Work 21 rows in g st. Cast/bind off.
Following the chart, Swiss darn a small heart motif in centre of st st panel using F.

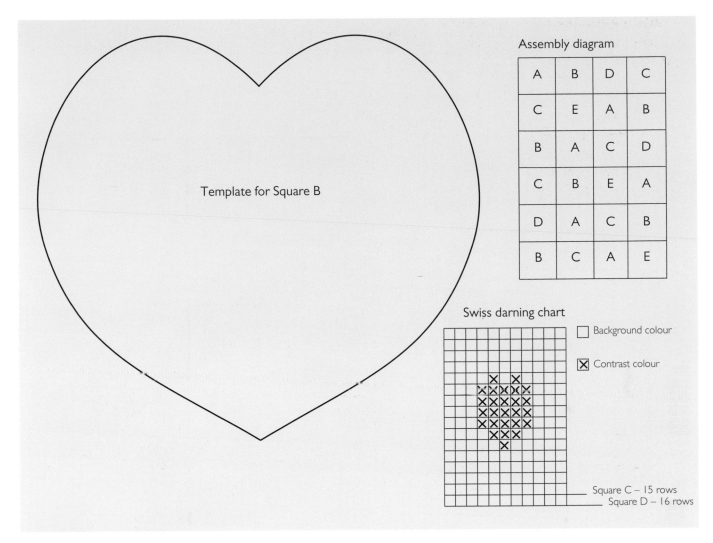

Template for Square B

Assembly diagram

A	B	D	C
C	E	A	B
B	A	C	D
C	B	E	A
D	A	C	B
B	C	A	E

Swiss darning chart

☐ Background colour

☒ Contrast colour

Square C – 15 rows
Square D – 16 rows

SQUARE E: (Make 3)
Using shade C, work as given for Square D.
Swiss darn heart motifs using D.

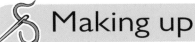 Making up

Using the assembly diagram as a guide, join the squares into six rows of four squares. Join the rows together, taking care to match the seams.

With 3.5mm (no. 9/US 4/E) crochet hook, C and RS of quilt facing, work 2 rounds of double (US single) crochet around outer edges, working approximately one double (US single) crochet into each st, one double (US single) crochet into every alternate row end and three double (US single) crochet in every corner.

Ruffle scarf

Make a statement with this extravagant scarf that has two giant ruffles running from top to bottom.

The Yarn
Debbie Bliss Cashmerino Aran is a blend of 55% merino wool with 33% microfibre and 12% cashmere to produce a yarn that is soft, luxurious and drapes well – perfect for glamorous accessories such as a scarf. There is a fabulous colour range with plenty of fashionable shades.

Pretty lacy ruffles are knitted onto either side of a straight ribbed strip for a flamboyant scarf that will add style to the plainest outfit.

GETTING STARTED

 Main part of scarf is simple double rib, but frills contain a large number of stitches and must be worked in a lacy pattern

Size:
Scarf is approximately 11cm wide x 146cm long (4¼in x 57½in), excluding frills

How much yarn:
6 x 50g (2oz) balls of Debbie Bliss Cashmerino Aran, approx 90m (98 yards) per ball

Needles:
*Pair of 4.5mm (no. 7/US 7) knitting needles
4mm (no. 8/US 6) and 5mm (no. 6/US 8) circular knitting needles*

Additional items:
Stitch markers

Tension/gauge:
*26 sts and 25 rows measures 10cm (4in) square over rib patt on 4.5mm (no. 7/US 7) needles
IT IS ESSENTIAL TO WORK TO THE STATED TENSION/ GAUGE TO ACHIEVE SUCCESS*

What you have to do:
Work main part (long strip) in k2, p2 rib with marked single stitches. Pick up loops along length of main part to make frills Use circular needles to knit frills in rows. Knit frills in a lace pattern, increasing to a large number of stitches.

Abbreviations:

alt = alternate;
beg = beginning;
cm = centimetre(s);
cont = continue;
foll = follows; **k** = knit;
p = purl; **patt** = pattern;
psso = pass slipped
stitch over;
RS = right side; **sl** = slip;
st(s) = stitch(es);
tog = together;
yfwd = yarn forward/yarn
over to make a stitch

Instructions

SCARF:
Main part:

With 4.5mm (no. 7/US 7) needles cast on 28 sts. Cont in rib patt.

1st row: (RS) (K2, p2) twice, k1 (mark this st), (p2, k2) twice, p2, k1 (mark this st), (p2, k2) twice.

2nd row: (P2, k2) twice, p1, (k2, p2) twice, k2, p1, (k2, p2) twice.

These 2 rows form rib patt. Patt 362 rows more. Cast/bind off.

Frills:

With 4mm (no. 8/US 6) circular needle and RS of main part facing, beg at cast-on edge and thread point of needle into centre of marked single k st on every alt row along one long side of main part, ending at cast/bound-off edge. 182 loops on needle. Work forwards and backwards in rows as foll: Join in yarn and k1 row. Change to 5mm (no. 6/US 8) circular needle. Cont in lace patt.

1st row: P2, (k1, yfwd, k1, yfwd, k1, p2) to end. 254 sts.

2nd row: K2, (p5, k2) to end.

3rd row: P2, (k1, yfwd, k3, yfwd, k1, p2) to end. 326 sts.

4th row: K2, (p7, k2) to end.

5th row: P2, (k1, yfwd, k2tog, yfwd, k1, yfwd, sl 1, k1, psso, yfwd, k1, p2) to end. 398 sts.

6th row: K2, (p9, k2) to end.

7th row: P2, (k1, yfwd, k2tog, yfwd, k3, yfwd, sl 1, k1, psso, yfwd, k1, p2) to end. 470 sts.

8th row: K2, (p11, k2) to end.

9th row: P2, (k1, yfwd, k2tog, yfwd, k2tog, yfwd, k1, yfwd, sl 1, k1, psso, yfwd, sl 1, k1, psso, yfwd, k1, p2) to end. 542 sts.

10th and 11th rows: With 4mm (no. 8/US 6) needles, k to end.

Cast/bind off knitwise.

Work 2nd frill in the same way, beg at cast/bound-off edge and working along 2nd marked single k st along other long side of main part.

HOW TO
MARK AND PICK UP STITCHES

The main fabric of this scarf is worked in a simple rib with stitches picked up and knitted on a circular needle to create the long frills.

1 Follow the pattern instructions to knit the main rib fabric of the scarf. Where instructed, slip a plastic stitch marker onto the stitches. You will end up with parallel lines of stitch markers along the length of the scarf, marking knit stitches on alternate rows.

2 Working from the cast-on edge of the scarf, slip the point of a circular needle into the centre of every marked stitch along one of the parallel lines of markers. You will have 182 loops on the needle.

3 Distribute the loops evenly around the circular needle. Join in the yarn and knit one row. Work the lace pattern as instructed and then cast/bind off knitwise. Pick up loops from the marked stitches along the second parallel line of markers and work the second frill.

Big cabled cardigan

This cardigan is designed on a giant scale; with extra large cable panels and knitted in a bold colour.

Comfortably slouchy, this very wide and short cable cardigan has intricate cable panels on the fronts and back. Knitted in a colourful, thick tweed yarn, it will be a delightful addition to your wardrobe for those cold days.

The Yarn

Debbie Bliss Donegal Luxury Tweed Chunky is a beautiful 100% pure wool in the classic tweed tradition. The weight makes it substantial for wearing outdoors and there is a fabulous shade range, that includes bright, contemporary colours, all bearing the subtle flecked appearance that characterizes tweed yarns.

Instructions

Abbreviations:

beg = beginning; **cn** = cable needle; **cont** = continue; **dec** = decrease(ing); **foll** = follow(s)(ing); **inc** = increase(ing); **k** = knit; **kfb** = k into front and back of st; **p** = purl; **patt** = pattern; **psso** = pass slipped stitch over; **rep** repeat; **RS** = right side; **sl** = slip; **st(s)** = stitch(es); **st st** = stocking/stockinette stitch; **tog** = together; **WS** = wrong side; **yo** = yarn over needle to make a stitch

C4BP = sl next st on to cn and hold at back, k3, p1 from cn
C4FP = sl next 3 sts on to cn and hold at front, p1, k3 from cn
C5BP = sl next 2 sts on to cn and hold at back, k3, p2 from cn
C5FP = sl next 3 sts on to cn and hold at front, p2, k3 from cn
C6B = sl next 3 sts on to cn and hold at back, k3, k3 from cn
C6F = sl next 3 sts on to cn and hold at front, k3, k3 from cn

CABLE PANEL: (Worked over 40 sts)

1st row: (RS) (P2, k3) twice, p7, k6, p7, (k3, p2) twice.
2nd and every WS row: K and p the sts as they appear
3rd row: P2, C4FP, C4BP, p7, C6F, p7, C4FP, C4BP, p2.
5th row: P3, C6F, p6, C5BP, C5FP, p6, C6F, p3.
7th row: P3, k3, C4FP, p3, C5BP, p4, C5FP, p3, C4BP, k3, p3.
9th row: P3, k3, p1, C4FP, C5BP, p8, C5FP, C4BP, p1, k3, p3.
11th row: P3, C5FP, C6B, p12, C6B, C5BP, p3.
13th row: P5, C6F, C5FP, p8, C5BP, C6F, p5.
15th row: P4, C4BP, (C5FP) twice, p4, (C5BP) twice, C4FP, p4.
17th row: P3, C4BP, p3, (C5FP) twice, (C5BP) twice, p3,

C4FP, p3.

19th row: P2, C4BP, p6, C5FP, C6F, C5BP, p6, C4FP, p2.

21st row: P2, k3, p9, (C6B) twice, p9, k3, p2.

23rd row: P2, k3, p9, k3, C6F, k3, p9, k3, p2.

25th row: P2, k3, p9, k12, p9, k3, p2.

27th row: As 23rd row.

29th row: As 21st row.

31st row: P2, C4FP, p6, C5BP, C6F, C5FP, p6, C4FP, p2.

33rd row: P3, C4FP, p3, (C5BP) twice, (C5FP) twice, p3, C4BP, p3.

35th row: P4, C4FP, (C5BP) twice, p4, (C5FP) twice, C4BP, p4.

37th row: P5, C6F, C5BP, p8, C5FP, C6F, p5.

39th row: P3, C5BP, C6B, p12, C6B, C5FP, p3.

41st row: P3, k3, p1, C4BP, C5FP, p8, C5BP, C4FP, p1, k3, p3.

43rd row: P3, k3, C4BP, p3, C5FP, p4, C5BP, p3, C4FP, k3, p3.

45th row: P3, C6F, p6, C5FP, C5BP, p6, C6F, p3.

47th row: P2, C4BP, C4FP, p7, C6F, p7, C4BP, C4FP, p2.

48th row: As 2nd row. These 48 rows form cable panel patt.

BACK:

With 5.5mm (no. 5/US 9) needles cast on 102 sts.

1st row: (RS) P2, (k3, p2) to end.

2nd row: K2, (p3, k2) to end.

These 2 rows form rib. Rib 7 more rows, ending with a RS row. K1 row.

Change to 7mm (no. 2/US 10½) needles.

1st row: (RS) K5, *(p2, k3) twice, p7, k2, sl 1, k1, psso, k2tog, k2, p7, (k3, p2) twice*, k8, rep from * to *, k5. 98 sts.

This row replaces 1st patt row and is not repeated.

2nd row: P5, *(k2, p3) twice, k7, p6, k7, (p3, k2) twice *, p8, rep from * to *, p5.

These 2 rows set position of two cable panels and form st st between and at each side. Noting that next row is 3rd row of cable panel, cont in patt for 14 more rows.

Inc row: (RS) K1, kfb, patt to last 3 sts, kfb, k2. 100 sts. Cont in patt, inc in this way at each end of 3 foll 6th rows. 106 sts. Patt 13 rows.

Shape armholes:

Cast/bind off 2 sts at beg of next 2 rows. 102 sts.

Dec row: (RS) K3, k2tog, patt to last 5 sts, sl 1, k1, psso, k3. 100 sts.

Cont in patt, dec in this way at each end of next 2 RS rows. 96 sts. Patt 33 rows, ending with 40th row of 2nd patt rep. Cast/bind off.

LEFT FRONT:

With 5.5mm (no. 5/US 9) needles cast on 51 sts.

1st row: (RS) (P2, k3) to last st, k1.

2nd row: P1, (p3, k2) to end.

These 2 rows form rib with 1 extra st at front edge. Rib 7 more rows, ending with a RS row. K1 row.

Change to 7mm (no. 2/US 10½) needles.

1st row: (RS) K5, (p2, k3) twice, p7, k2, sl 1, k1, psso, k2tog, k2, p7, (k3, p2) twice, k4. 49 sts.

This row replaces 1st patt row and is not repeated.

2nd row: P4, (k2, p3) twice, k7, p6, k7, (p3, k2) twice, p5.

These 2 rows set position of cable panel and form st st at each side. Noting that next row is 3rd row of cable panel, cont in patt for 14 more rows.

Inc row: (RS) K1, kfb, patt to end. 50 sts. Cont in patt, inc in this way at beg of 3 foll 6th rows. 53 sts. Patt 13 rows.

Shape armhole:

Cast/bind off 2 sts at beg of next row. 51 sts. Patt 1 row.

Dec row: (RS) K3, k2tog, patt to end. 50 sts.

Cont in patt, dec in this way at beg of next 2 RS rows. 48 sts. Patt 19 rows, ending with 26th row of 2nd patt rep.

Shape neck:

Next row: (RS) Patt 37, turn and leave 11 sts on a holder for neck. Cont in patt, dec 1 st at neck edge on next 12 rows. 25 sts. Patt 1 row. Cast/bind off.

RIGHT FRONT:

With 5.5mm (no. 5/US 9) needles cast on 51 sts.

1st row: (RS) K1, (k3, p2) to end.

2nd row: (K2, p3) to last st, p1.

These 2 rows form rib with 1 extra st at front edge. Rib 7 more rows, ending with a RS row. K 1 row.

Change to 7mm (no. 2/US 10½) needles.

1st row: (RS) K4, (p2, k3) twice, p7, k2, sl 1, k1, psso, k2tog, k2, p7, (k3, p2) twice, k5. 49 sts.

This row replaces 1st patt row and is not repeated.

2nd row: P5, (k2, p3) twice, k7, p6, k7, (p3, k2) twice, p4.

These 2 rows set position of cable panel and form st st at each side. Noting that next row is 3rd row of cable panel, cont in patt for 14 more rows.

Inc row: (RS) Patt to last 3 sts, kfb, k2. 50 sts.

Cont in patt, inc in this way at end of 3 foll 6th rows. 53 sts. Patt 14 rows.

Shape armhole:

Cast/bind off 2 sts at beg of next row. 51 sts.

Dec row: (RS) Patt to last 5 sts, sl 1, k1, psso, k3. 50 sts.

Cont in patt, dec in this way at end of next 2 RS rows. 48 sts. Patt 19 rows, ending with 26th row of 2nd patt rep.

Shape neck:

Next row: (RS) Patt 11 and leave these 11 sts on a holder for neck, patt to end. 37 sts.

Cont in patt, dec 1 st at neck edge on next 12 rows. 25 sts. Patt 1 row. Cast/bind off.

SLEEVES:

With 5.5mm (no. 5/US 9) needles cast on 37 sts. Work 9 rows in rib as given for Back. K1 row.

Change to 7mm (no. 2/US 10½) needles. Beg with a k row, work 2 rows in st st.

Inc row: (RS) K1, kfb, k to last 3 sts, kfb, k2. 39 sts.

Cont in st st, inc in this way at each end of 7 foll 8th rows. 53 sts. Work 7 rows in st st.

Shape top:

Cast/bind off 2 sts at beg of next 2 rows. 49 sts.

Dec row: (RS) K1, k2tog, k to last 3 sts, sl 1, k1, psso, k1. 47 sts.

Dec in this way at each end of next 2 RS rows. 43 sts. P1 row. Cast/bind off.

NECKBAND:

Join shoulder seams.

With 5.5mm (no. 5/US 9) needles and RS facing, sl 11 sts from right front holder, allowing cables to fold to pick up 3 sts from each strand of the plait/braid and picking up extra sts from between and at each side to fit patt to p2, k3 rib, pick up and k15 sts up right front neck, k48 sts across back neck, 15 sts down left front neck, (p2, k3) twice, k1 from holder. 100 sts. K1 row. Cont in rib as foll:

1st row: (RS) K4, (p2, k3) to last st, k1.

2nd row: P4, (k2, p3) to last st, p1.

These 2 rows form rib with 1 extra st at each end. Work 2 more rows.

Next row: (RS) K2tog, k2, (p2tog, k3) 18 times, p2tog, k2, sl 1, k1, psso. 79 sts.

Cast/bind off knitwise.

BUTTON BAND:

With 5.5mm (no. 5/US 9) needles and RS facing, pick up and k 62 sts down left front edge. K1 row.

Cont in rib as foll:

1st row: (RS) K5, (p2, k3) to last 2 sts, k2.

2nd row: K2, (p3, k2) to end.

These 2 rows form rib with k2 at each end on every row **. Work 5 more rows. Cast/bind off knitwise.

BUTTONHOLE BAND:

Work as given for Button band to **.

Buttonhole row: (RS) K2, rib 7, sl 1, k1, psso, (yo) twice, k2tog, * rib 11, sl 1, k1, psso, (yo) twice, k2tog, rep from * two more times, k4.

Next row: K2, p3, (* k into back of first yo, drop 2nd yo, then pick it up again with left needle so strand faces the opposite way and k into front of it *, rib 13) 3 times, rep from * to *, rib 8, k2.

Work 3 more rows. Cast/bind off knitwise.

✄ Making up

Press according to directions on ball band. Set in sleeves. Join side and sleeve seams. Sew on buttons.

Garden cushion

Put this colourful cushion/pillow on a garden bench or step
to make an impromptu seat while you admire the view.

Enhance a quiet spot with a comfortable seat worked in a colourful variety of patterns – vertical stripes, zig-zags and spots – all created with the easy-to-knit slip stitch method.

GETTING STARTED

 The patterns may be easy, but for a neat finish care must be taken with sewing up

Size:
Cushion/pillow is 34cm x 60cm x 6cm (13½in x 24 x 2½in)

How much yarn:
5 x 50g (2oz) balls Debbie Bliss Cotton DK, approx 84m (92 yards) per ball, in colour A, 5 balls in colour B, 1 ball in colour C, 2 balls in colour D and 1 ball in colour E

Needles:
Pair of 4mm (no. 8/US 6) knitting needles

Additional items:
Foam pad 34cm x 60cm x 6cm (13½in x 24in x 2½in)
Yarn needle

Tension/gauge:
21 sts and 23 rows measure 10cm (4in) square over stripe patt worked on 4mm (no. 8/US 6) needles
IT IS ESSENTIAL TO WORK TO THE STATED TENSION/GAUGE TO ACHIEVE SUCCESS

What you have to do:
Work straight pieces of fabric in coloured patterns using slip stitch as described in instructions. Carefully join together from the right side using mattress stitch.

The Yarn
Debbie Bliss Cotton DK is a pure cotton yarn with a matt finish. It is available in a wide range of fabulous colours that are ideal for mix and match patterns such as those used in the cushion/pillow.

Instructions

Abbreviations:
beg = beginning; **cm** = centimetre(s); **cont** = continue; **foll** = follows; **k** = knit; **p** = purl; **patt** = pattern; **rep** = repeat; **RS** = right side; **sl** = slip purlwise; **st(s)** = stitch(es); **st st** = stocking/stockinette stitch; **tog** = together; **WS** = wrong side

TOP AND BOTTOM PIECES: (Make 2)
With A, cast on 72 sts. P1 row. Cont in stripe patt as foll:
1st row: (RS) With B, k1, *sl 2 with yarn at back, k2, rep from * to last 3 sts, sl 2, k1.
2nd row: With B, k1, *sl 2 with yarn at front, p2, rep from * to last 3 sts, sl 2, p1.
3rd row: With A, k1, *k2, sl 2 with yarn at back, rep from * to last 3 sts, k3.
4th row: With A, k1, *p2, sl 2 with yarn at front, rep from * to last 3 sts, p2, k1.
Rep these 4 rows until work measures 61cm (24in) from beg, ending with a WS row. Cut off B. Cast/bind off knitwise, using A.

END PIECES: (Make 2)
With E, cast on 74 sts. P1 row. Cont in zig-zag patt as foll:
1st row: (RS) With B, k1, *sl1, k2, rep from * to last st, k1.
2nd row: With B, k1, *p2, sl1, rep from * to last st, k1.
3rd row: With E, k1, *k1, sl1, (k2, Sl1) 3 times, k3, (Sl1, k2) 3 times, Sl1, rep from * to last st, k1.
4th row: With E, k1, *Sl1, (p2, Sl1) 3 times, p3, (Sl1, p2) 3 times, Sl1, p1, rep from * to last st, k1.
5th row: With B, k1, *k2, (Sl1, k2) 3 times, Sl1, k1, Sl1, (k2, Sl1) 3 times, k1, rep from * to last st, k1.
6th row: With B, k1, *p1, (Sl1, p2) 3 times, Sl1, p1, Sl1, (p2, Sl1) 3 times, p2, rep from * to last st, k1.

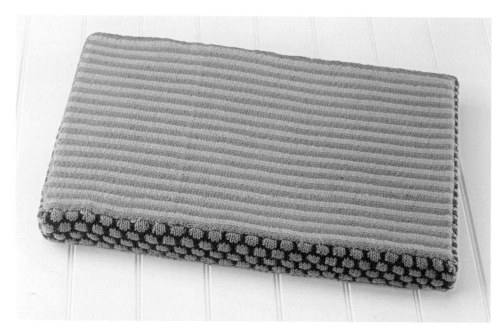

7th and 8th rows: With E instead of B, rep 1st and 2nd rows.

9th and 10th rows: With B instead of E, rep 3rd and 4th rows.

11th and 12th rows: With E instead of B, rep 5th and 6th rows.

Rep these 12 rows until work measures 6.5cm (2½in) from beg, ending with a WS row. Cut off B. Cast/bind off knitwise, using E.

SIDE PIECES: (Make 2)

With C, cast on 97 sts. Cont in spot patt as foll:

1st row: (WS) With C, p to end.

2nd–5th rows: With D and beg with a k row, work 4 rows in st st.

6th row: With C, k2, *drop next st off needle and unravel 4 rows down, picking up st in C from 1st row, insert needle into this st and under 4 loose strands of D and k, catching loose strands behind st, k3, rep from * ending with k2 instead of k3.

7th row: With C, p to end.

8th–11th rows: As 2nd–5th rows.

12th row: With C, k4, *drop next st, unravel and k st in C from 5th row below as given in 6th row, k3, rep from * to last st, k1.

Rep these 12 rows until work measures 6.5cm (2½in) from beg, ending with a WS row. Cut off D. Cast/bind off knitwise, using C.

HOW TO
SEW UP USING MATTRESS STITCH

To join the pieces for the cushion you need to lay them over the cut foam block, right side up, and pin in place. Join the pieces using mattress stitch.

2 Take the needle back to the right-hand piece and bring it up under the edge of the two stitches. Now take the needle back to the left-hand piece, insert it back into the stitch that the yarn is emerging from and take the needle up and under the next two stitches.

1 Secure the bottom edges of the seam with a figure-of-eight stitch. Take the needle across and under the left-hand piece and bring it through to the front from the same hole as the securing stitch.

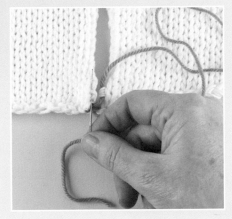

3 Continue working from side to side in this way, tightening the yarn every few stitches to pull the two pieces together. When you reach the top of the seam, secure the yarn and trim off the end.

Making up

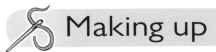

Block and press pieces to correct size. Cut the foam block to measure 34 x 60 x 6cm (13½in x 24 x 2½in). Pin pieces into place on the block. Using A and mattress stitch, join top and side pieces together first, pressing seams as you work for a neat finish. Join vertical seams of end and side pieces together with mattress stitch and then join end pieces to top. Sew bottom piece in place.

Tips

• When sewing up, choose the same colour that most of the pattern is worked in.

• For a professional, neat finish, make sure that you join pieces in the same direction – with the cast-on edge at the bottom and the cast/bound-off edge at the top.

Cable tote bag

Practise your cabling skills with this tweedy bag that's perfect for work or shopping.

With its rich Aran cables and textures knitted in a traditional tweed yarn, this trendy tote will make a useful accessory that is good to look at as well.

The Yarn

Debbie Bliss Donegal Luxury Tweed Aran is a luxurious blend of 85% wool and 15% angora. It is available in a range of traditional heathery shades with subtle flecks of colour and can be hand washed if necessary.

GETTING STARTED

 Keeping track of three different cable panels could be difficult but knitted pieces are straight

Size:
Bag is 36cm wide x 39cm deep (16in x 15½in), excluding handles

How much yarn:
6 x 50g (2oz) balls of Debbie Bliss Donegal Luxury Tweed Aran, approx 88m (96 yards) per ball

Needles:
Pair of 5mm (no. 6/US 8) knitting needles, Cable needle

Additional items:
44cm x 80cm (17½in x 31½in) needlecord fabric for lining

Matching sewing cotton and needle
1m (1 yard) of webbing for handles, 2.5cm (1in) wide

Tension/gauge:
16 sts and 26 rows measure 10cm (4in) square over double moss/seed st on 5mm (no. 6/US 8) needles
IT IS ESSENTIAL TO WORK TO THE STATED TENSION/GAUGE TO ACHIEVE SUCCESS

What you have to do:
Work in cable panels with double moss/seed stitch at each end. Sew up bag, curving corners. Sew on webbing handles. Stitch fabric lining, then insert and secure in bag.

Instructions

Abbreviations:

cn = cable needle; **cont** = continue; **dec** = decrease; **foll** = follows; **inc** = increase; **k** = knit; **p** = purl; **patt** = pattern; **psso** = pass slipped stitch over; **rep** = repeat; **RS** = right side; **sl** = slip; **st(s)** = stitch(es); **tbl** = through back of loops; **tog** = together; **WS** = wrong side

C6B = sl next 3 sts on to cn and hold at back, k3, then k3 from cn

C6F = sl next 3 sts on to cn and hold at front, k3, then k3 from cn

C8F = sl next 4 sts on to cn and hold at front, k4, then k4 from cn

MB = k into front, back and front of next st, turn and p3, turn and inc in first st, k1, inc in last st, turn and p5, turn and k2tog tbl, k1, k2tog, turn and p3, turn and sl 1, k2tog, psso

CABLE A: (Worked over 13 sts)
1st row: (WS) K2, p9, k2.
2nd row: P2, k9, p2.
3rd row: As 1st row.
4th row: P2, C6B, k3, p2.
5th and 6th rows: As 1st and 2nd rows.
7th row: As 1st row.
8th row: P2, k3, C6F, p2.
9th row: As 1st row.
The 2nd–9th rows form patt.
For Bag, work 1st–9th rows, (2nd–9th rows) 10
times and then 2nd–7th rows. 95 rows in total.

CABLE B: (Worked over 24 sts)
1st row: (WS) P2, k6, p8, k6, p2.
2nd row: K2, p6, k8, p6, k2.
3rd and 4th rows: As 1st and 2nd rows.
5th row: P2, k5, p5, k1, p4, k5, p2.
6th row: K2, p5, k5, p1, k4, p5, k2.
7th row: P2, k4, p4, (k1, p1) twice, p4, k4, p2.
8th row: K2, p4, k4, (p1, k1) twice, k4, p4, k2.
9th row: P2, k3, p4, (p1, k1) 3 times, p4, k3, p2.
10th row: K2, p3, k4, (k1, p1) 3 times, k4, p3, k2.
11th row: P2, k2, p4, (k1, p1) 4 times, p4, k2, p2.
12th row: K2, p2, k4, (p1, k1) 4 times, k4, p2, k2.
13th row: P2, k1, p4, (p1, k1) 5 times, p4, k1, p2.
14th row: K2, p1, k4, (k1, p1) 5 times, k4, p1, k2.
15th row: As 13th row.
16th row: K2, p1, k4, (k1, p1) twice, MB, p1, (k1, p1)
twice, k4, p1, k2.
17th–20th rows: Rep 13th and 14th rows twice.
21st and 22nd rows: As 11th and 12th rows.
23rd and 24th rows: As 9th and 10th rows.
25th and 26th rows: As 7th and 8th rows.
27th and 28th rows: As 5th and 6th rows.
29th and 30th rows: As 1st and 2nd rows.
31st row: As 1st row.
32nd row: K2, p6, C8F, p6, k2.
33rd and 34th rows: As 1st and 2nd rows.
35th row: As 1st row.
The 4th–35th rows form patt. For Bag, rep 1st–35th rows,
4th–35th rows and then 4th–31st rows.
95 rows in total.

CABLE C: (Worked over 13 sts)
1st row: (WS) K2, p9, k2.
2nd row: P2, k9, p2.
3rd row: As 1st row.

4th row: P2, k3, C6F, p2.
5th and 6th rows: As 1st and 2nd rows.
7th row: As 1st row.
8th row: P2, C6B, k3, p2.
9th row: As 1st row.
The 2nd –9th rows form patt. For Bag, work 1st–9th rows, (2nd–9th rows) 10 times and then 2nd–7th rows. 95 rows in total.

DOUBLE MOSS/SEED STITCH:

(Worked over 9 sts)
1st row: (WS) K1, (p1, k1) 4 times.
2nd row: K1, (p1, k1) 4 times.
3rd row: P1, (k1, p1) 4 times.
4th row: As 3rd row.
5th row: As 2nd row.
The 2nd–5th rows form patt. For Bag, rep these 4 rows throughout.

BAG FRONT:

With 5mm (no. 6/US 8) needles cast on 68 sts. Cont in patt with cable panels A, B, C and double moss/seed st at sides, placing panels as foll:
1st row: (WS) Work 9 sts as 1st row double moss/seed st, 13 sts as 1st row Cable C, 24 sts as 1st row Cable B, 13 sts as 1st row Cable A, 9 sts as 1st row double moss/seed st.
Cont in patt as set until 95 rows in all have been completed, ending with a WS row and dec 1 st in centre of last row. 67 sts.
Next row: (RS) (K1, p1) to last st, k1.
Next row: (P1, k1) to last st, p1.
Rep last 2 rows once more, then work 1st of them again. Cast/bind off knitwise.

BAG BACK:

Work as given for Front.

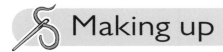

Making up

Press pieces according to directions on ball band, taking care not to flatten pattern. Place front and back with RS facing, and pin around three sides to form bag. At corners, mark 8cm (3in) from corner on each seam, then draw a curve linking the two marks. Backstitch seams and around curved corners. Trim curved corners (as bag is lined and knitting dense, the fabric will not unravel) and turn bag RS out. Press seams.
Cut two 38cm x 44cm (15in x 17½in) pieces of fabric (this

includes 1cm (⅜in) seam allowance at each side and 4cm (1½in) around top opening). Curve lower corners as given for bag, then with RS facing, stitch seams. Turn 4cm (1½in) around top edge to WS and press. Leave lining WS out. Cut two 46cm (18in) lengths of webbing for handles. Pin one handle on front, placing 8cm (3in) to WS of front at plait/braid cable on either side of main cable. Hand stitch securely in place. Insert lining into bag so that top edge is about 1cm (⅜in) below bag opening and slip stitch neatly in place.

Hot-water bottle cover

Knit this amazingly soft cover and your hot-water bottle will become your new best friend.

Snuggle up to this cosy hot-water bottle cover knitted in easy moss/seed stitch and trimmed with blanket stitch embroidery and pompoms.

The Yarn
Debbie Bliss Cashmerino Aran is a super-soft blend of merino wool with microfibre and cashmere – just perfect for cuddling up to. The silky-smooth yarn highlights the texture of the moss/seed stitch pattern and there is a comprehensive colour range to choose from.

GETTING STARTED

Easy moss/seed stitch with some simple shaping

Size:
To fit standard size hot-water bottle

How much yarn:
3 x 50g (2oz) balls of Debbie Bliss Cashmerino Aran, approx 90m (98 yards) per ball, in main shade MS
1 ball in contrast colour C

Needles:
Pair of 5mm (no. 6/US 8) knitting needles

Additional items:
5 buttons

Tension/gauge:
18 sts and 31 rows measure 10cm (4in) square over moss/seed st on 5mm (no. 6/US 8) needles
IT IS ESSENTIAL TO WORK TO THE STATED TENSION/GAUGE TO ACHIEVE SUCCESS

What you have to do:
Work in moss/seed stitch. Simple increasing and decreasing. Make eyelet buttonholes and openings for cord. Decorate with blanket stitch. Make a twisted cord and decorate with pompoms.

 Instructions

Abbreviations:
alt = alternate; **beg** = beginning; **cont** = continue; **dec** = decrease(ing); **foll** = following; **inc** = increase(ing); **k** = knit; **p** = purl; **rep** = repeat; **RS** = right side; **st(s)** = stitch(es); **tog** = together; **WS** = wrong side; **yfwd** = yarn forward/yarn over

FRONT:

With MS, cast on 29 sts.

1st row: (RS) P1, *k1, p1, rep from * to end.

Rep this row to form moss/seed st.

Cont in moss/seed st, work

1 row, then inc 1 st at each end of next 3 rows, then at each end of foll 3 alt rows, working extra sts in moss/seed st. 41 sts.**

Work 67 rows without shaping, ending with a WS row.

***Keeping moss/seed st correct, dec 1 st at each end of next and foll 2 alt rows, then at each end of next 3 rows, ending with a WS row. 29 sts. Cast/bind off 3 sts at beg of next 4 rows. 17 sts.

Eyelet row: (RS) P1, k1, (yfwd, k2tog, p1, k1) 3 times, yfwd, k2tog, p1.

Work 3 rows, then inc 1 st at each end of next and foll 4th row. 21 sts. Work 13 rows straight, ending with a WS row. Cast/bind off in moss/seed st.

LOWER BACK:

Work as given for Front to **.

Work 35 rows straight, ending with a WS row. Insert a marker at each end of last row. Work 8 more rows, ending with a WS row. Cast/bind off in moss/seed st.

UPPER BACK:

With MS, cast on 41 sts.

Work 4 rows in moss/seed st as given for Front, ending with a WS row.

Buttonhole row: (RS) (P1, k1) twice, *yfwd, k2tog, (p1, k1) 3 times, rep from * 3 times more, yfwd, k2tog, p1, k1, p1.

Work 3 rows, ending with a WS row. Insert a marker at each end of last row. Work 24 rows straight, ending with a WS row. Complete as given for Front from *** to end.

 Making up

Do not press.
Lay Upper back over Lower back so that markers on Upper back match cast/bound-off edge of Lower back and markers on Lower back match cast-on edge of Upper back. Oversew overlapped edges together at side seams. Sew on buttons to correspond with buttonholes. With right sides facing and using backstitch, join front and back together around outer edges, leaving cast/bound-off edges (upper edge) open. Turn to right side through back opening. Using C, embroider blanket stitch around the upper edge.

Using C, make a twisted cord about 85cm (34in) long and thread through eyelet holes, starting and ending at centre front.
Using C, make 2 pompoms (see page 31), each 6cm (2½in) in diameter, and attach one to each end of cord. Tie cord in a bow at centre front.

Long textured scarf

Light yet warm, this openwork scarf will become one of your favourite winter woollies.

No winter outfit is complete without an extra-long scarf in an interesting fabric. This one features an unusual texture with openwork and bobbles.

The Yarn

Debbie Bliss Cashmerino Chunky is a mixture of 55% merino wool, 33% microfibre and 12% cashmere. It has a matt sheen and is super-soft and warm, so perfect for a scarf. There are plenty of colours to choose from, including strong dark shades as well as contemporary pastels.

GETTING STARTED

Chunky yarn is easy to knit but keeping the pattern correct requires concentration

Size:
Scarf is 20cm wide x 192cm long (8in x 75in)

How much yarn:
7 x 50g (2oz) balls of Debbie Bliss Cashmerino Chunky, approx 65m (71 yards) per ball

Needles:
Pair of 6mm (no. 4/US 10) knitting needles

Tension/gauge:
19 sts and 20 rows measure 10cm (4in) square over patt on 6mm (no. 4/US 10) needles
IT IS ESSENTIAL TO WORK TO THE STATED TENSION/ GAUGE TO ACHIEVE SUCCESS

What you have to do:
Work beginning and end of scarf in moss/seed stitch. Work main pattern in openwork fabric with bobble texture following the instructions.

Abbreviations:

cm = centimetre(s);
cont = continue;
dec = decrease;
foll = follows;
inc = increase;
k = knit; **p** = purl;
patt = pattern;
rep = repeat;
RS = right side;
st(s) = stitch(es);
tog = together;
yfwd = yarn forward/yarn
over to make a stitch

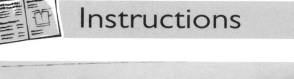

Instructions

SCARF:

Cast on 33 sts.

Next row: (RS) K1, *p1, k1, rep from * to end.
Rep this row to form moss/seed st. Work 4 more rows
in moss/seed st.

Inc row: K6, (k1, p1, k1) all into next st, *k9, (k1, p1, k1) all
into next st, rep from * once more, k6. 39 sts.
Cont in patt as foll:

1st–4th rows: K1, *k1, yfwd, k4, k3tog, k4, yfwd, rep from
* twice more, k2.

5th–8th rows: K1, p2tog, *k4, yfwd, k1, yfwd, k4, p3tog,
rep from * once more, k4, yfwd, k1, yfwd, k4, p2tog, k1.
Rep these 8 rows 46 times more (work measures
approximately 190cm (75in) when laid flat or there is
about 6m (6 yards) left on last ball of yarn), ending with an
8th patt row.

Dec row: (RS) K6, k3tog, *k9, k3tog, rep from * once
more, k6. 33 sts.
Work 5 rows in moss/seed st. Cast/bind off in moss/seed
st.

HOW TO
WORK THE OPENWORK PATTERN

The pattern is worked over eight rows and these are repeated forty-six times to give the completed length. A moss/seed stitch border is worked at the beginning and end of the scarf.

I Cast on 33 stitches. On the first row, which is the right side, knit one and then purl one and knit one to the end of the row. Repeat this row four more times to create the moss/seed stitch border. On the next row, knit six and then knit one, purl one and knit one into the next stitch. Work a sequence of knit nine and then knit one, purl one, and knit one into the next stitch and repeat this sequence once more. Knit the last six stitches. You will now have thirty-nine stitches.

2 The next row is the first row of the openwork pattern. Begin with knit one and then work a sequence of knit one, yarn forward/yarn over, knit four, knit three together, knit four and yarn forward/yarn over. Repeat this sequence twice more and then knit the last two stitches.

3 Repeat this row three more times.

4 For the fifth row, knit one and purl two together. Work a sequence of knit four, yarn forward/yarn over, knit one, yarn forward/yarn over, knit four and purl three together. Repeat this sequence again. Then knit four, yarn forward/yarn over, knit one, yarn forward/yarn over, knit four, purl two together and knit one. Repeat this row three more times to complete the first eight-row pattern repeat. Repeat these eight rows forty-six times more and then work a decrease row and five rows in moss/seed stitch to complete the scarf.

Chunky rib and cable sweater

The ribs and cable pattern in this sweater are certainly man-sized, but the chunky yarn helps to make it a speedy knit.

Sort out his weekend wear with this chunky cable-patterned sweater featuring a zipped neck opening and easy-fitting raglan sleeves.

The Yarn

King Cole Maxi-Lite Chunky is 72% acrylic, 3% polyester and 25% wool. It is lightweight and ideal for a bulky man's garment. The sweater can also be machine washed and there are plenty of contemporary colours to choose from, including some variegated shades.

GETTING STARTED

Chunky yarn knits up quickly but cables will take some concentration

Size:
To fit chest: 97–102[107–112:117–122]cm/38–40[42–44:46–48]in
Actual size: 104[116:128]cm/41[45½:50]in
Length: 76[77.5:81]cm/30[30½:32]in
Sleeve seam: 48[51:53]cm/19[20:21]in
Note: *Figures in square brackets [ ] refer to larger sizes; where there is only one set of figures, it applies to all sizes*

How much yarn:
9[10:11] x 100g (3½oz) balls of King Cole Maxi-Lite Chunky, approx 100m (109 yards) per ball

Needles:
Pair of 10mm (no. 000/US 15) knitting needles
Cable needle

Additional items:
Stitch holders, Zip fastener, 20cm (8in) long

Tension/gauge:
10 sts and 14 rows measure 10cm (4in) square over rib patt on 10mm (no. 000/US 15) needles
IT IS ESSENTIAL TO WORK TO THE STATED TENSION/GAUGE TO ACHIEVE SUCCESS

What you have to do:
Work in wide rib pattern with cable panels. Work styled shaping for raglan armholes. Leave centre front neck opening, working each side separately. Pick up stitches from around neck to work k1, p1 neckband. Sew in zip fastener.

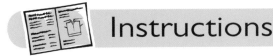

Instructions

Abbreviations:

alt = alternate; **beg** = beginning; **cm** = centimetre(s); **cont** = continue; **C6F** = sl next 3 sts on to a cable needle and leave at front of work, k3, then k 3 sts from cable needle; **dec** = decrease(ing); **foll** = follow(s)(ing); **inc** = increase; **k** = knit; **p** = purl; **patt** = pattern; **psso** = pass slipped stitch over; **rem** = remain; **rep** = repeat; **RS** = right side; **sl** = slip; **st(s)** = stitch(es); **tbl** = through back of loops; **tog** = together; **WS** = wrong side

BACK:

With 10mm (no. 000/US 15) needles and thumb method, cast on 58[64:70] sts. Cont in rib patt with cables as foll:
1st row: (RS) P0[1:0], k4[6:2], (p2, k6) 6[7:8] times, p2[1:2], k4[0:2].
2nd row: K0[1:0], p4[6:2], (k2, p6) 6[7:8] times, k2[1:2], p4[0:2].
3rd and 4th rows: As 1st and 2nd rows.
5th row: P0[1:0], k4[6:2], (p2, k6) 2[2:3] times, (p2, C6F) twice, (p2, k6) 2[2:3] times, p2[1:2], k4[0:2].
6th row: As 2nd rows.
7th and 8th rows: As 1st and 2nd rows.

Rep these 8 rows to form patt until work measures 47[47:49] cm/18½[18½:19¼]in from beg, ending with a WS row.

Shape raglan armholes:
Cast/bind off 4 sts at beg of next 2 rows. 50[56:62] sts.

1st and 2nd sizes only:
1st row: K1, sl 1, k1, psso, patt to last 3 sts, k2tog, k1.
2nd row: P2, patt to last 2 sts, p2.
3rd row: K2, patt to last 2 sts, k2.
4th row: P2, patt to last 2 sts, p2.
These 4 rows set raglan shaping.
Rep them 1[0] times more.
46[54] sts.

3rd size only:
1st row: K1, sl 1, psso, patt to last 3 sts, k2tog, k1.
2nd row: P1, p2tog, patt to last 3 sts, p2tog tbl, p1. 58 sts.

All sizes:
1st row: K1, sl 1, k1 psso, patt to last 3 sts, k2tog, k1.
2nd row: P2, patt to last 2 sts, p2. ** Cont to dec 1 st at each end of next and every foll alt row to 22[24:24] sts, ending with a WS row. Cut off yarn and leave rem sts on a holder.

FRONT:
Work as given for Back to **. Work 2[8:12] rows, dec 1 st at each end of next and every foll alt row. 42[44:44] sts.

Divide for opening:
Next row: K1, sl 1, k1, psso, patt 18[19:19] sts, turn and leave rem sts on a holder.
Complete this side of opening first. Work 12 rows, dec 1 st at raglan edge in every foll alt row. 14[15:15] sts.

Shape neck:
Next row: Cast/bind off 6[7:7] sts, patt to end. 8 sts.
Work 2 rows, dec 1 st as before at raglan edge in 1st row and 1 st at neck edge in both rows. 5 sts.
Next row: K1, sl 1, k1, psso, k2tog. 3 sts.
Next row: P to end.
Next row: K1, sl 1, k1, psso. 2 sts.
Next row: P2tog and fasten off.
With RS of work facing, rejoin yarn to rem 21[22:22] sts on holder, patt to last 3 sts, k2tog, k1. Work 11 rows, dec 1 st as before at raglan edge in every foll alt row. 15[16:16] sts.

Shape neck:
Next row: Cast/bind off 6[7:7] sts, patt to last 3 sts, k2tog,

k1. 8 sts. Work 3 rows, dec 1 st as before at raglan edge in 2nd row and 1 st at neck edge in 1st and 2nd rows. 5 sts.
Next row: (K2tog) twice, k1. 3 sts.
Next row: P to end.
Next row: K2tog, k1. 2 sts.
Next row: P2tog and fasten off.

SLEEVES:

With 10mm (no. 000/US 15) needles and thumb method, cast on 34[36:38] sts. Cont in rib patt with cables as foll:
1st row: (RS) K0[1:2], (p2, k6) 4 times, p2, k0[1:2].
2nd row: P0[1:2], (k2, p6) 4 times, k2, p0[1:2].
3rd and 4th rows: As 1st and 2nd rows.
5th row: K0[1:2], p2, k6, (p2, C6F) twice, p2, k6, p2, k0[1:2].
6th row: As 2nd rows.
7th and 8th rows: As 1st and 2nd rows.
These 8 rows set patt. Keeping patt correct, inc 1 st at each end of next and every foll 10th[8th:8th] row until there are 46[44:54] sts, working extra sts into patt.

2nd size only:
Inc 1 st at each end of every foll 10th row until there are 50 sts.

All sizes:
Work straight until Sleeve measures 48[51:53]cm/19[20:21] in from beg, ending with a WS row.

Shape raglan top:
Cast/bind off 4 sts at beg of next 2 rows. 38[42:46] sts.
1st row: K1, sl 1, k1, psso, patt to last 3 sts, k2tog, k1.
2nd row: P2, patt to last 2 sts, p2.
3rd row: K2, patt to last 2 sts, k2.
4th row: P2, patt to last 2 sts, p2.
These 4 rows set raglan shaping. Work 16[12:8] rows, dec 1 st at each end of next and every foll 4th row. 28[34:40] sts. Cont to dec 1 st at each end of next and every foll alt row to 16 sts, ending with a WS row. Cut off yarn and leave rem 16 sts on a holder.

NECKBAND:

Join raglan seams.
With 10mm (no. 000/US15) needles and RS of work facing, pick up and k9[10:10] sts along right side of neck, work across 16 sts at top of right sleeve as foll: k1, (k2tog) 3 times, k2, (k2tog) 3 times, k1, work across 22[24:24] back neck sts as foll: k1[2:2], k2tog, (k1, k2tog) 6 times, k1[2:2], work across 16 sts at top of left sleeve as foll: k1, (k2tog) 3 times, k2, (k2tog) 3 times, k1, then pick up and k9[10:10] sts along left side of neck. 53[57:57] sts.
1st row: K1, *k1, p1, rep from * to last 2 sts, k2.

2nd row: P1, *p1, k1, rep from * to last 2 sts, p2.
Work 9 more rows in rib as set. Cast/bind off in rib.

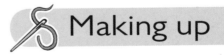 Making up

Join side and sleeve seams. Sew in zip fastener.

Folk-art cushion

Traditional colours and embroidered motifs give this cushion/pillow a homely, folksy appeal.

Worked in stocking/stockinette stitch with a reverse stocking/stockinette stitch back, the colours and simple stylized floral pattern are reminiscent of folk art. Curving lines of stems and leaves are embroidered on afterwards.

The Yarn
Debbie Bliss Fez is 85% wool and 15% camel and has a soft, slightly felted appearance. It can be hand washed and there is a good range of solid colours to choose from.

GETTING STARTED

 Working colour patterns from a chart takes some practise

Size:
Cushion/pillow is 38cm (15in) square

How much yarn:
4 x 50g (2oz) balls of Debbie Bliss Fez, approx 100m (109 yards) per ball, in colour A
1 ball in colour B

Needles:
Pair of 5mm (no. 6/US 8) knitting needles

Additional items:
1 x 10m skein of Anchor tapestry wool
Blunt-ended wool needle
40cm (16in) square cushion pad/pillow form

Tension/gauge:
17 sts and 21 rows measure 10cm (4in) square over st st on 5mm (no. 6/US 8) needles
IT IS ESSENTIAL TO WORK TO THE STATED TENSION/GAUGE TO ACHIEVE SUCCESS

What you have to do:
Work front in stocking/stockinette stitch and back in reverse stocking/stockinette stitch. Work coloured motifs on front using intarsia and Fair Isle techniques. Follow chart to work colour pattern. Use simple embroidery to embellish finished front.

Abbreviations:

beg = beginning;
cm = centimetre(s);
cont = continue;
foll = follows; **k** = knit;
p = purl; **patt** = pattern;
rep = repeat;
RS = right side;
st(s) = stitch(es);
st st = stocking/
stockinette stitch;
tog = together;
WS = wrong side

Note: Work motifs on Front in B using the intarsia technique with a separate small ball of yarn (or wind yarn on to bobbins) for each one. Twist yarns tog at edges of motifs when changing colours to prevent holes from forming. When working motifs, strand or weave colour A across the WS of the work.

Instructions

FRONT:

With A, cast on 65 sts. Beg with a k row, cont in st st and work 10 rows. Join in B. Cont in st st, work in patt from chart as foll:

1st row: (RS) K7 B,
k across 30 sts of 1st row of chart reading from right to left, then rep 21 motif sts again reading from left to right, k7 B.

2nd row: P7 B, p across 21 motif sts of 2nd row of chart, reading from right to left, then p across 30 sts of 2nd row of chart reading from left to right, p7 B.

Cont in patt as set from chart until 61 rows have been completed. Cut off B. Cont in A, work 10 more rows, ending with a RS row. Cast/bind off.

BACK PANELS:
Top section:

With A, cast on 65 sts. Beg with a p row, cont in reverse st st until work measures 23cm (9in) from beg, ending with a k row. Work opening edge as foll:

Next row: (RS) K to end.
Next row: K1, (p1, k1) to end.
Next row: K to end.
Next row: P1, (k1, p1) to end.
Rep last 4 rows twice more. Cast/bind off.
Bottom section:
Work as given for Top section until work measures 18cm (7in) from beg, ending with a k row. Work 2 rows as given for opening edge of Top section. Cast/bind off.

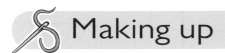 ## Making up

Press according to directions on ball band. Using green tapestry wool, embroider chain stitch lines between motifs on front, as shown in photographs. Keep the chain stitches fairly large and even. Work leaves (groups of three lazy daisy stitches) at intervals as shown.
Lay the cushion/pillow front with right side facing up. Place the top section and then bottom section of back panels on top, with right sides facing down and overlapping opening edges in the centre. Join together by backstitching around outer edges. Turn right side out through back opening. Insert cushion pad/pillow form.

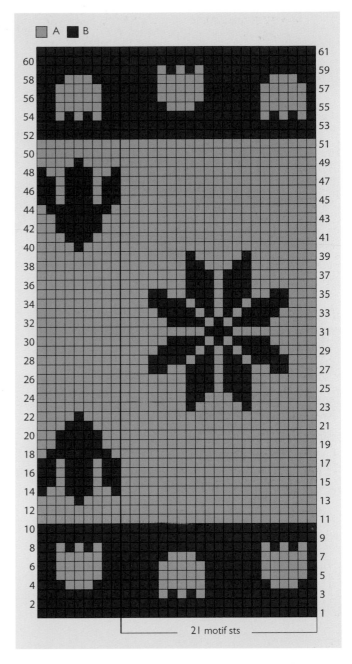

□ A ■ B

21 motif sts

Guernsey sweater

Traditional styling and patterns make this a classic sweater for all occasions.

The focal point of this long-line stocking/stockinette stitch sweater is an intricate pattern of textured stitches and cable panels around the lower half.

GETTING STARTED

Top half is straightforward, but the patchwork pattern requires skill

Size:
To fit bust: *81–86[91–97:102–107]cm/ 32–34[36–38:40–42]in*
Actual size: *91[102:112.5]cm/36[40:44]in*
Length: *72[74:77]cm/28[29:30]in*
Sleeve seam: *46[46:46]cm/18[18:18]in*
Note: *Figures in square brackets [ ] refer to larger sizes; where there is only one set of figures, it applies to all sizes*

How much yarn:
6[6:7] x 100g (3½oz) balls of King Cole Bamboo Cotton DK, approx 230m (252 yards) per ball

Needles:
Pair of 3.25mm (no. 10/US 3) knitting needles
Pair of 4mm (no. 8/US 6) knitting needles
Cable needle

Additional items:
Stitch holders

Tension/gauge:
22 sts and 28 rows measure 10cm (4in) square over st st on 4mm (no. 8/US 6) needles
IT IS ESSENTIAL TO WORK TO THE STATED TENSION/GAUGE TO ACHIEVE SUCCESS

What you have to do:
Work lower edge, cuffs and neckband in double (knit two, purl two) rib. Work lower section of sweater front and back in lattice and trellis textured patchwork pattern. Work remainder of sweater in stocking/stockinette stitch, using simple shaping. Pick up stitches around neckline, work neckband.

The Yarn

King Cole Bamboo Cotton DK contains 50% bamboo and 50% cotton. It is a fantastic yarn for summer sweaters and it can be machine washed at a low temperature. There is a small range of classic and contemporary colours to choose from.

Abbreviations:

alt = alternate;
beg = beginning;
cm = centimetre(s);
cn = cable needle;
cont = continue;
dec = decrease(ing);
foll = follow(s)(ing);
inc = increase(ing);
k = knit;
p = purl; **patt** = pattern;
rem = remain(ing);
RS = right side; **sl** = slip;
st(s) = stitch(es);
st st = stocking/
stockinette stitch;
tog = together;
WS = wrong side
C6B = cable 6 back as foll:
sl next 3 sts on to cn and
leave at back of work, k3,
then k 3 sts from cn
C6F = cable 6 front as foll:
sl next 3 sts on to cn and
leave at front of work, k3,
then k 3 sts from cn
Cr2L = cross 2 left as foll:
sl next st on to cn and leave
at front of work, k1, then k
1 st from cn
Cr2R = cross 2 right as foll:
sl next st on to cn and leave
at back of work, k1, then k 1
st from cn
Tw2L = twist 2 left as foll:
sl next st on to cn and leave
at front of work, p1, then k
1 st from cn
Tw2R = twist 2 right as
foll: sl next st on to cn and
leave at back of work, k1,
then p 1 st from cn

Instructions

BACK:

With 3.25mm (no. 10/US 3) needles and thumb method, cast on 102[114:126] sts.
1st row: (RS) K2, (p2, k2) to end.
2nd row: P2, (k2, p2) to end. Work 7 more rows in rib as set, ending with a RS row.
Next row: Rib 9[15:21], inc in next st, rib 3, inc in next st, rib 74, inc in next st, rib 3, inc in next st, rib 9[15:21]. 106[118:130] sts. Change to 4mm (no. 8/US 6) needles. Cont in patt as foll:
1st row: *(P1, k1) 3[6:9] times, p2, k9, (p6, Cr2R) 4 times, p5*, k15, p1, k1, p1, k15, p2, k9, p2, (k1, p1) 3[6:9] times.
2nd row: (K1, p1) 3[6:9] times, k2, p9, k2, p14, k2, p1, k2, p14, *k5, (p2, k6) 4 times, p9, k2, (p1, k1) 3[6:9] times.*
3rd row: *(K1, p1) 3[6:9] times, p2, C6B, k3, p5, (Tw2R, Tw2L, p4) 4 times*, k13, p2, k3, p2, k13, p2, C6B, k3, p2, (p1, k1) 3[6:9] times.
4th row: (P1, k1) 3[6:9] times, k2, p9, k2, p12, k2, p5, k2, p12, (k4, p1, k2, p1) 4 times, k5, p9, k2, (k1, p1) 3[6:9] times.
5th row: (P1, k1) 3[6:9] times, p2, k9, p4, (Tw2R, p2, Tw2L, p2) 4 times, p1, k11, p2, k2, p1, k1, p1, k2, p2, k11, p2, k9, p2, (k1, p1) 3[6:9] times.

6th row: (K1, p1) 3[6:9] times, k2, p9, k2, p10, k2, p2, k2, p1, k2, p2, k2, p10,*k3, (p1, k4, p1, k2) 4 times, k2, p9, k2, (p1, k1) 3[6:9] times.*
7th row: *(K1, p1) 3[6:9] times, p2, k3, C6F, p3, (Tw2R, p4, Tw2L) 4 times, p2*, k9, p2, k2, p2, k3, p2, k2, p2, k9, p2, k3, C6F, p2, (p1, k1) 3[6:9] times.
8th row: (P1, k1) 3[6:9] times, k2, p9, k2, p8, k2, p2, k2, p5, k2, p2, k2, p8, *k2, (p1, k6, p1) 4 times, k3, p9, k2, (k1, p1) 3[6:9] times.*
9th row: *(P1, k1) 3[6:9] times, p2, k9, p3, k1, (p6, Cr2L) 3 times, p6, k1, p2*, k7, (p2, k2) twice, p1, k1, p1, (k2, p2) twice, k7, p2, k9, p2, (k1, p1) 3[6:9] times.
10th row: (K1, p1) 3[6:9] times, k2, p9, k2, p7, k1, (p2, k2) twice, p1, (k2, p2) twice, k1, p7, *k2, (p1, k6, p1) 4 times, k3, p9, k2, (p1, k1) 3[6:9] times.*
11th row: *(K1, p1) 3[6:9] times, p2, C6B, k3, p3, (Tw2L, p4, Tw2R) 4 times, p2*, k9, p2, k2, p2, k3, p2, k2, p2, k9, p2, C6B, k3, p2, (p1, k1) 3[6:9] times.
12th row: (P1, k1) 3[6:9] times, k2, p9, k2, p8, k2, p2, k2, p5, k2, p2, k2, p8, *k3, (p1, k4, p1, k2) 4 times, k2, p9, k2, (k1, p1) 3[6:9] times.*

13th row: *(P1, k1) 3[6:9] times, p2, k9, p4, (Tw2L, p2, Tw2R, p2) 4 times, p1*, k8, (p1, k2, p2, k2, p1, k1) twice, k7, p2, k9, p2, (k1, p1) 3[6:9] times.

14th row: (K1, p1) 3[6:9] times, k2, p9, k2, p10, k2, p2, k2, p1, k2, p2, k2, p10, *(k4, p1, k2, p1) 4 times, k5, p9, k2, (p1, k1) 3[6:9] times.*

15th row: *(K1, p1) 3[6:9] times, p2, k3, C6F, p5, (Tw2L, Tw2R, p4) 4 times, * k9, p2, k2, p2, k3, p2, k2, p2, k9, p2, k3, C6F, p2, (p1, k1) 3[6:9] times.

16th row: (P1, k1) 3[6:9] times, (k2, p9) twice, k1, p2, k2, p5, k2, p2, k1, p9, k5, (p2, k6) 4 times, p9, k2, (k1, p1) 3[6:9] times.

17th row: Work from * to * as given for 1st row, k11, p2, k2, p1, k1, p1, k2, p2, k11, p2, k9, p2, (k1, p1) 3[6:9] times.

18th row: (K1, p1) 3[6:9] times, k2, p9, k2, p10, k2, p2, k2, p1, k2, p2, k2, p10, work from * to * as given for 2nd row.

19th row: Work from * to * as given for 3rd row, k10, p1, k2, p2, k3, p2, k2, p1, k10, p2, C6B, k3, p2, (p1, k1) 3[6:9] times.

20th row: As 4th row.

21st row: As 5th row.

22nd row: (K1, p1) 3[6:9] times, k2, p9, k2, p11, k1, p2, k2, p1, k2, p2, k1, p11, work from * to * as given for 6th row.

23rd row: Work from * to * as given for 7th row, k13, p2, k3, p2, k13, p2, k3, C6F, p2, (p1, k1) 3[6:9] times.

24th row: (P1, k1) 3[6:9] times, k2, p9, k2, p12, k2, p5, k2, p12, work from * to * as given for 8th row.

25th row: Work from * to * as given for 9th row, k12, p1, k2, p1, k1, p1, k2, p1, k12, p2, k9, p2, (k1, p1) 3[6:9] times.

26th row: (K1, p1) 3[6:9] times, k2, p9, k2, p14, k2, p1, k2, p14, work from * to * as given for 10th row.

27th row: Work from * to * as given for 11th row, k13, p2, k3, p2, k13, p2, C6B, k3, p2, (p1, k1) 3[6:9] times.

28th row: (P1, k1) 3[6:9] times, k2, p9, k2, p13, k1, p5, k1, p13, work from * to * as given for 12th row.

29th row: Work from * to * as given for 13th row, k13, p2, k3, p2, k13, p2, k9, p2, (k1, p1) 3[6:9] times.

30th row: (K1, p1) 3[6:9] times, k2, p9, k2, p14, k2, p1, k2, p14, work from * to * as given for 14th row.

31st row: Work from * to * as given for 15th row, k15, p1, k1, p1, k15, p2, k9, p2, k3, C6F, p2, (p1, k1) 3[6:9] times.

32nd row: (P1, k1) 3[6:9] times, k2, p9, k2, p33, k5, (p2, k6) 4 times, p9, k2, (k1, p1) 3[6:9] times.

33rd row: (P1, k1) 3[6:9] times, p2, k9, p72, k9, p2, (k1, p1) 3[6:9] times.

34th row: (K1, p1) 3[6:9] times, k2, p9, k72, p9, k2, (p1, k1) 3[6:9] times.

35th row: (K1, p1) 3[6:9] times, p2, C6B, k3, p2, k15, p1, k1, p1, k15, *p5, (Cr2R, p6) 4 times, C6B, k3, p2, (p1, k1)

3[6:9] times.*

36th row: *(P1, k1) 3[6:9] times, k2, p9, (k6, p2) 4 times, k5*, p14, k2, p1, k2, p14, k2, p9, k2, (k1, p1) 3[6:9] times.

37th row: (P1, k1) 3[6:9] times, p2, k9, p2, k13, p2, k3, p2, k13, *(p4, Tw2R, Tw2L) 4 times, p5, k9, p2, (k1, p1) 3[6:9] times. *

38th row: (K1, p1) 3[6:9] times, k2, p9, k5, (p1, k2, p1, k4) 4 times, p12, k2, p5, k2, p12, k2, p9, k2, (p1, k1) 3[6:9] times.

39th row: (K1, p1) 3[6:9] times, p2, k3, C6F, p2, k11, p2, k2, p1, k1, p1, k2, p2, k11, p3, (Tw2R, p2, Tw2L, p2) 4 times, p2, k3, C6F, p2, (p1, k1) 3[6:9] times.

40th row: *(P1, k1) 3[6:9] times, k2, p9, k4, (p1, k4, p1, k2) 4 times, k1*, p10, k2, p2, k2, p1, k2, p2, k2, p10, k2, p9, k2, (k1, p1) 3[6:9] times.

41st row: (P1, k1) 3[6:9] times, (p2, k9) twice, p2, k2, p2, k3, p2, k2, p2, k9, *p2, (Tw2R, p4, Tw2L) 4 times, p3, k9, p2, (k1, p1) 3[6:9] times.*

42nd row: *(K1, p1) 3[6:9] times, k2, p9, k3, (p1, k6, p1) 4 times, k2*, p8, k2, p2, k2, p5, k2, p2, k2, p8, k2, p9, k2, (p1, k1) 3[6:9] times.

43rd row: (K1, p1) 3[6:9] times, p2, C6B, k3, p2, k7, (p2, k2) twice, p1, k1, p1, (k2, p2) twice, k7, *p2, k1, (p6, Cr2L) 3 times, p6, k1, p3, C6B, k3, p2, (p1, k1) 3[6:9] times.*

44th row: *(P1, k1) 3[6:9] times, k2, p9, k3, (p1, k6, p1) 4 times, k2*, p7, k1, (p2, k2) twice, p1, (k2, p2) twice, k1, p7, k2, p9, k2, (k1, p1) 3[6:9] times.

45th row: (P1, k1) 3[6:9] times, (p2, k9) twice, p2, k2, p2, k3, p2, k2, p2, k9, *p2, (Tw2L, p4, Tw2R) 4 times, p3, k9, p2, (k1, p1) 3[6:9] times. *

46th row: *(K1, p1) 3[6:9] times, k2, p9, k4, (p1, k4, p1, k2) 4 times, k1*, p8, k2, p2, k2, p5, k2, p2, k2, p8, k2, p9, k2, (p1, k1) 3[6:9] times.

47th row: (K1, p1) 3[6:9] times, p2, k3, C6F, p2, k8, (p1, k2, p2, k2, p1, k1) twice, k7, *p3, (Tw2L, p2, Tw2R, p2) 4 times, p2, k3, C6F, p2, (p1, k1) 3[6:9] times. *

48th row: * (P1, k1) 3[6:9] times, k2, p9, k5, (p1, k2, p1, k4) 4 times*, p10, k2, p2, k2, p1, k2, p2, k2, p10, k2, p9, k2, (k1, p1) 3[6:9] times.

49th row: (P1, k1) 3[6:9] times, (p2, k9) twice, (p2, k2, p2, k3) twice, k6, *(p4, Tw2L, Tw2R) 4 times, p5, k9, p2, (k1, p1) 3[6:9] times. *

50th row: (K1, p1) 3[6:9] times, k2, p9, (k6, p2) 4 times, k5, p9, k1, p2, k2, p5, k2, p2, k1, (p9, k2) twice, (p1, k1) 3[6:9] times.

51st row: (K1, p1) 3[6:9] times, p2, C6B, k3, p2, k11, p2, k2, p1, k1, p1, k2, p2, k11, work from * to * as given for 35th row.

52nd row: Work from * to * as given for 36th row, p10, k2, p2, k2, p1, k2, p2, k2, p10, k2, p9, k2, (k1, p1) 3[6:9] times.

53rd row: (P1, k1) 3[6:9] times, p2, k9, p2, k10, p1, k2, p2, k3, p2, k2, p1, k10, work from * to * as given for 37th row.

54th row: As 38th row.

55th row: As 39th row.

56th row: Work from * to * as given for 40th row, p11, k1, p2, k2, p1, k2, p2, k1, p11, k2, p9, k2, (k1, p1) 3[6:9] times.

57th row: (P1, k1) 3[6:9] times, p2, k9, p2, k13, p2, k3, p2, k13, work from * to * as given for 41st row.

58th row: Work from * to * as given for 42nd row, p12, k2, p5, k2, p12, k2, p9, k2, (p1, k1) 3[6:9] times.

59th row: (K1, p1) 3[6:9] times, p2, C6B, k3, p2, k12, p1, k2, p1, k1, p1, k2, p1, k12, work from * to * as given for 43rd row.

60th row: Work from * to * as given for 44th row, p14, k2, p1, k2, p14, k2, p9, k2, (k1, p1) 3[6:9] times.

61st row: (P1, k1) 3[6:9] times, p2, k9, p2, k13, p2, k3, p2, k13, work from * to * as given for 45th row.

62nd row: Work from * to * as given for 46th row, p13, k1, p5, k1, p13, k2, p9, k2, (p1, k1) 3[6:9] times.

63rd row: (K1, p1) 3[6:9] times, p2, k3, C6F, p2, k13, p2, k3, p2, k13, work from * to * as given for 47th row.

64th row: Work from * to * as given for 48th row, p14, k2, p1, k2, p14, k2, p9, k2, (k1, p1) 3[6:9] times.

65th row: (P1, k1) 3[6:9] times, p2, k9, p2, k15, p1, k1, p1, k15, work from * to * as given for 49th row.

66th row: (K1, p1) 3[6:9] times, k2, p9, (k6, p2) 4 times, k5, p33, k2, p9, k2, (p1, k1) 3[6:9] times.

Next row: P9[15:21], p2tog, p3, p2tog, p74, p2tog, p3, p2tog, p9[15:21]. 102[114:126] sts.

Next row: K to end. Beg with a k row, cont working in st st until Back measures 53[53:54]cm/21[21:21¼]in, ending with a WS row.

Shape armholes:

Cast/bind off 6 sts at beg of next 2 rows. 90[102:114] sts.**

Cont without shaping until armholes measure 19[21:23]cm/ 7½[8¼:9]in, ending with a WS row.

Shape shoulders:

Cast/bind off 14[17:20] sts at beg of next 2 rows and 15[17:20] sts at beg of foll 2 rows. Cut off yarn and leave rem 32[34:34] sts on holder.

FRONT:

Work as given for Back to **.

Cont without shaping until armholes measure 11[12:14]cm/ 4¼[4¾:5½]in, ending with a WS row.

Shape neck:

Next row: K35[40:46], turn and complete this side of neck first.

Next row: P to end.

Dec 1 st at neck edge on next 3 rows, then on every foll alt row until 29[34:40] sts rem. Cont without shaping until armhole measures 19[21:23]cm/ 7½[8¼:9]in, ending at armhole edge.

Shape shoulder:

Cast/bind off 14[17:20] sts at beg of next row. Work 1 row, then Cast/bind off rem 15[17:20] sts.

With RS of work facing, sl centre 20[22:22] sts on to a holder, rejoin yarn to rem 35[40:46] sts and k to end.

Next row: P to end.

Complete as given for first side of neck.

SLEEVES:

With 3.25mm (no. 10/US 3) needles and thumb method, cast on 54[58:58] sts. Work 10 rows in k2, p2 rib as given for Back. Change to 4mm (no. 8/US 6) needles. Beg with a k row, cont in st st, inc 1 st at each end of 7th and every foll 8th[8th:6th] row until there are 76[80:88] sts, then at each end of every foll 10th[10th:8th] row until there are 80[84:92] sts. Work straight until Sleeve measures 46cm (18in), ending with a WS row. Insert markers at each end of last row, then work 6 rows more.

Shape top:

Cast/bind off 8[8:9] sts at beg of next 4 rows and 8[9:10] sts at beg of foll 4 rows. Cast/bind off rem 16 sts.

NECKBAND:

Join right shoulder seam.

With 3.25mm (no. 10/US 3) needles and RS of work facing, pick up and k 25[25:27] sts evenly along left side of neck, k across 20[22:22] front neck sts on holder, pick up and k 25[25:27] sts evenly along right side of neck and k across 32[34:34] back neck sts on holder. 102[106:110] sts. Beg with 2nd row of k2, p2 rib, cont in rib until Neckband measures 8cm 3in), ending with a WS row. Cast/bind off in rib.

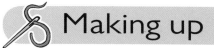

Making up

Join left shoulder and neckband seam. Fold sleeves in half lengthways, then place fold to shoulder seam and rows above markers to cast/bound-off sts on back and front, and sew sleeves in position. Join side and sleeve seams.

Extra-long scarf

A favourite accessory, this scarf makes a great present for the man in your life.

This colourful scarf, worked in a wide rib pattern, is long enough to wind around your neck again and again, and still have long trailing ends.

The Yarn

Debbie Bliss Cashmerino Aran is a mixture of 55% merino wool, 33% microfibre and 12% cashmere. It produces a soft and cosy fabric for a scarf and there are plenty of colours to choose from for the stripe patterns.

Instructions

Abbreviations:

beg = beginning; **cm** = centimetre(s); **cont** = continue; **foll** = follows; **k** = knit; **p** = purl; **patt** = pattern; **rep** = repeat; **RS** = right side; **st(s)** = stitch(es)

SCARF:

With A, cast on 60 sts.

1st row: (RS) K4, *p4, k4, rep from * to end.
2nd row: P4, *k4, p4, rep from * to end.

Cont in rib patt as set, work 10 more rows. Cut off A and join in B. K 1 row, then beg with 2nd row, work 39 rows in patt. Cut off B and join in C. K 1 row, then beg with 2nd row, work 7 rows in patt. Cont in patt (always k first row of colour change), working in colour sequence as foll:

D for 20 rows;
E for 8 rows;
D for 14 rows;
B for 22 rows;
C for 10 rows;
A for 54 rows;
E for 10 rows;
D for 18 rows;
E for 10 rows**;
B for 44 rows;
C for 12 rows;
B for 8 rows;
D for 16 rows;

GETTING STARTED

This is a good project for a beginner but it will take time to finish as there is a lot of knitting

Size:

Scarf is approximately 27cm wide x 3m long (10½in x 118in)

How much yarn:

4 x 50g (2oz) balls of Debbie Bliss Cashmerino Aran, approx 90m (98 yards) per ball, in each of three colours A, B and D
2 balls in each of two colours C and E

Needles:

Pair of 5mm (no. 6/US 8) knitting needles

Tension/gauge:

22 sts and 25 rows measure 10cm (4in) square over rib patt stretched on 5mm (no. 6/US 8) needles
IT IS ESSENTIAL TO WORK TO THE STATED TENSION/ GAUGE TO ACHIEVE SUCCESS

What you have to do:

Work in knit four, purl four rib pattern. Join in colours as required, cutting off previous colour. Always knit first row of each new stripe to create a smooth line of colour.

A for 30 rows;
D for 8 rows;
B for 22 rows;
D for 44 rows;
C for 8 rows;
D for 22 rows;
E for 10 rows;
B for 16 rows;
A for 52 rows;
C for 8 rows.
Return to start of sequence (i.e. A for 12 rows) and rep colour sequence to **. Cast/bind off in patt.

 Making up

Darn in all cut ends of yarn carefully, working into a row of the same colour.

BEGINNERS' STITCH GUIDE

KNIT FOUR, PURL FOUR RIB

Worked over an even number of stitches, this rib makes a flat, elastic fabric that is perfect for a scarf. To work the rib, on the first row, which is the right side, knit four and then repeat a sequence of purl four and knit four to the end of the row. For the second row, purl four and then repeat a sequence of knit four and purl four to the end of the row. These two rows form the pattern and are repeated until you reach the desired length.

Super-chunky throw

Quick to knit and cosy to snuggle up with, this is the ultimate mini throw.

This throw, knitted in a super-thick yarn, is bound with glamorous sheer ribbon in a matching colour.

GETTING STARTED

Easy with no shaping and, although quite large, it is quick to make because the yarn is very thick

Size:
Throw is approximately 100cm x 110cm (39in x 43in)

How much yarn:
9 x 100g (3½oz) hanks of Colinette Point Five, approx 50m (54 yards) per hank

Needles:
Pair of 12mm (no. 0000/US 17) knitting needles

Additional items:
4.5m (5 yards) of matching ribbon
Sewing needle and matching thread

Tension/gauge:
7.5 sts and 10 rows measure 10cm (4in) square over patt on 12mm (no. 0000/US 17) needles
IT IS ESSENTIAL TO WORK TO THE STATED TENSION/ GAUGE TO ACHIEVE SUCCESS

What you have to do:
Cast on. Work rows of knit and purl to form simple pattern. Cast/bind off. Bind the edges with ribbon.

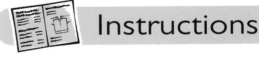 Instructions

The Yarn
This highly textured and super-thick yarn is 100% pure wool. It is called Point Five from Colinette and it knits up very quickly. There is a vast selection of variegated shades in fantastic colour combinations that produce fabulous fabrics in even the most simple stitches.

Abbreviations:
k = knit; **p** = purl; **patt** = pattern; **rep** = repeat; **st(s)** = stitch(es)

THE THROW:
Cast on 75 sts.
1st row: K to end.
2nd row: P to end.
3rd row: P to end.
4th row: K to end.
Rep these 4 rows to form patt until work measures 110cm (43in) from cast-on edge, ending with a 4th row. Cast/bind off.

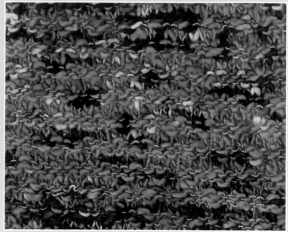

BEGINNERS' STITCH GUIDE

KNIT AND PURL PATTERN

Varying the sequence in which you knit simple knit and purl rows gives an interesting and straightforward pattern. Here you work a knit row followed by a purl row, which gives two rows of stocking/stockinette stitch, but this is followed by another purl row, which creates a garter-stitch ridge, and a knit row. This row sequence makes the pattern reversible.

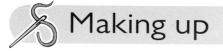 Making up

Sew in all the loose ends of yarn. Lay the throw on a flat surface (possibly the floor), smooth out to the finished size and pin the edges if possible. Press with a warm iron over a slightly damp cloth.

Sewing on ribbon: Fold ribbon in half lengthways and press to mark the crease line. Adding a 1cm (⅜in) seam allowance at each end, mark the corner points at 100cm (39in), 110cm (43in), 100cm (39in) and 110cm (43in). Taking 1cm (⅜in) seam allowance, sew ends of ribbon together to form a continuous loop. Pin the corner points in position at the appropriate corners,

sandwiching the knitting between the two layers of folded ribbon. Pin free edge of ribbon in place along all four sides. At each corner, work a line of small gathering stitches along each free inner edge. Draw up the gathering stitches so that ribbon fits around corner and pin in place. Repeat on the other side. Using small running stitch and matching sewing thread, stitch ribbon in place along inner edge, working through all three layers and repeat on the other side of the throw.

HOW TO
USE BIG NEEDLES

Some beginners love using big needles and yarn because all the stitches are magnified and the knitting grows very quickly, while others find the size of the needles difficult to master. Here are some tips for using big needles and thick yarn.

1 Try holding the right-hand needle with your hand over the needle rather than trying to hold it in a pen grip with the needle resting between your thumb and forefinger.

2 Hold both the needles in your left hand while you wind the yarn around the needle to form the stitch. Large needles are not heavy so you can do this quite easily.

3 Make sure that you keep the stitches on both needles near to the tip of the needles as you work. This means that as you make the stitches and lift them from one needle to the other, your movements can be kept small. Stop and slide the stitches forward as needed.

Patterned-stripe sweater

This soft, cuddly sweater has stripes of Fair Isle pattern that add colour interest and a challenge for the knitter.

Loose and casual with drop shoulders and rolled edges, this sweater looks elegantly stylish in a softly brushed yarn with interesting patterned stripes of complementary colours.

The Yarn
Rowan Alpaca Cotton contains 72% alpaca and 28% cotton. Softly shaded with a brushed appearance from the alpaca fibres, it is available in a range of muted colours. Rowan Pure Wool Aran contains 100% wool and there is a wide range of shades that are ideal for colour work.

GETTING STARTED

This style of sweater requires minimum shaping and is easy to knit in stocking/stockinette stitch, but working patterned stripes requires concentration

Size:
To fit bust: *81[86:91:97:102]cm/32[34:36:38:40]in*
Actual size: *96[101:105:110:115]cm/37¾ [39¾:41¼:43¼:45¼]in*
Length (before rolling up): *71[71:71:72:72] cm/28[28:28:28½:28½]in*
Sleeve seam (before rolling up): *50cm (20in)*
Note: *Figures in square brackets [ ] refer to larger sizes; where there is only one set of figures, it applies to all sizes*

How much yarn:
6[6:6:7:7] x 50g (2oz) balls of Rowan alpaca Cotton, approx 135m (148 yards) per ball, in main colour M
1 x 100g (3½oz) ball of Rowan Pure Wool Aran, approx 170m (186 yards) per ball, in contrast colour A
2 x 100g (3½oz) ball of Rowan Pure Wool Aran in contrast colour B
1 x 100g (3½oz) ball of Rowan Pure Wool Aran in contrast colour C

Needles:
Pair of 4.5mm (no. 7/US 7) knitting needles
Pair of 5mm (no. 6/US 8) knitting needles
Pair of 5.5mm (no. 5/US 9) knitting needles

Tension/gauge:
17 sts and 22 rows measure 10cm (4in) square over st st with Allegra on 5mm (no. 6/US 8) needles
IT IS ESSENTIAL TO WORK TO THE STATED TENSION/GAUGE TO ACHIEVE SUCCESS

What you have to do:
Work main fabric in stocking/stockinette stitch throughout. Follow charts to work stripes with Fair Isle patterns at intervals. When working stripes, carry colour not in use across wrong side of work. Pick up stitches around neckline to work rolled neckband.

Instructions

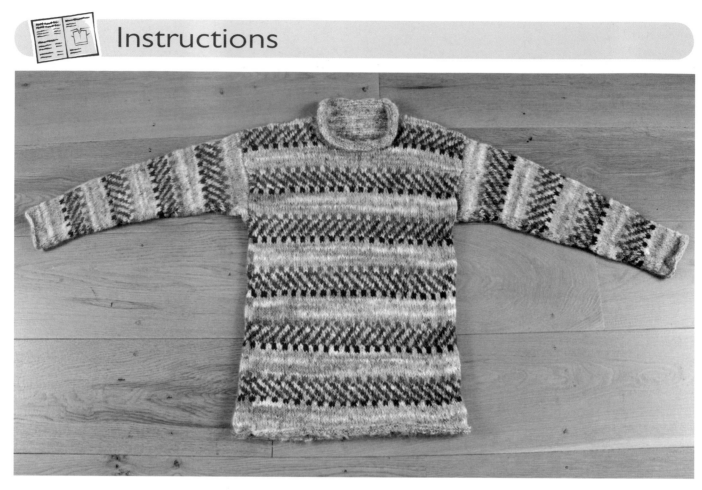

Abbreviations:

alt = alternate; **beg** = beginning; **cm** = centimetre(s);
cont = continue; **dec** = decrease(ing); **foll** = following;
inc = increase(ing); **k** = knit; **p** = purl; **patt** = pattern;
rem = remain(ing); **rep** = repeat; **RS** = right side;
sl = slip; **st(s)** = stitch(es); **st st** = stocking/stockinette
stitch; **WS** = wrong side

BACK:

With 4.5mm (no. 7/US 7) needles and M, cast on
82[86:90:94:98] sts. Beg with a k row, work 3 rows in st st.
Change to 5mm (no. 6/US 8) needles. Beg with a p row,
cont in st st for 15 more rows.

Change to 5.5mm (no. 5/US 9) needles. Cont in st st and
joining in A, B and C as required, work 10 rows in patt
from Chart 1, reading odd-numbered (k) rows from right
to left and even-numbered (p) rows from left to right and
carrying colour not in use loosely across WS of work.

Change to 5mm (no. 6/US 8) needles. Cont in M only and
beg with a k row, work 10 rows in st st.

Change to 5.5mm (no. 5/US 9) needles. Cont in st st, work
10 rows in patt as before from Chart 2.

Change to 5mm (no. 6/US 8) needles. Cont in M only and
beg with a k row, work 10 rows in st st. The last 40 rows
form patt. Rep them until work measures 71[71:71:72:72]
cm 28[28:28:28½:28½]in from beg, ending with a p row.

Shape shoulders:

Cast/bind off 9[10:10:11:11] sts at beg of next 4 rows and
10[9:11:10:12] sts at beg of foll 2 rows. Cut off yarn. Leave
rem 26[28:28:30:30] sts on a holder.

FRONT:

Work as given for Back until there are 12[14:14:14:16]
rows less than Back to shoulders, ending with a p row.

Shape neck:

Next row: Patt 33[34:36:37:39] sts, turn.
Complete this side of neck first. Dec 1 st at neck edge on
next 3 rows, then on 2 foll alt rows. 28[29:31:32:34] sts.
Work straight to match Back to shoulder, ending at
side edge.

Shape shoulder:

Cast/bind off 9[10:10:11:11] sts at beg of next and foll alt
row. Work 1 row. Cast/bind off rem 10[9:11:10:12] sts.
With RS facing, sl centre 16[18:18:20:20] sts on to a holder,
rejoin yarn to next st and patt to end. Complete to match
first side of neck.

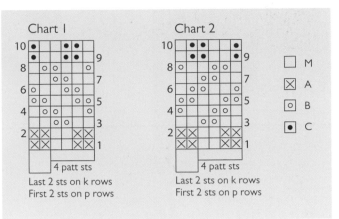

SLEEVES: (Make 2)

With 4.5mm (no. 7/US 7) needles and M, cast on 34[38:38:42:42] sts. Beg with a k row, work 3 rows in st st. Change to 5mm (no. 6/US 8) needles. Beg with a p row, cont in st st, inc 1 st at each end of foll 10th row and then on foll 4th row. 38[42:42:46:46] sts. P 1 row.

Change to 5.5mm (no. 5/US 9) needles. Cont in patt from Chart 1, work 2 rows. Using 5.5mm (no. 5/US 9) needles for 2-colour rows and 5mm (no. 6/US 8) needles for remainder, cont in patt as before, inc 1 st at each end of next and every foll 4th row until there are 56[54:66:64:76] sts, then at each end of every foll 6th row until there are 68[70:74:76:80] sts. Work straight until Sleeve measures 50cm (20in) from beg, ending with a p row. Cast/bind off loosely in M.

NECKBAND:

Join left shoulder seam.

With 4.5mm (no. 7/US 7) needles, M and RS of work facing, pick up and k across 26[28:28:30:30] back neck sts on holder, pick up and k 14[16:16:16:18] sts down left front

neck, k across 16[18:18:20:20] front neck sts on holder and pick up and k14[16:16:16:18] sts up right front neck. 70[78:78:82:86] sts.

Change to 5mm (no. 6/US 8) needles. Beg with a p row, work 10 rows in st st. Change to 4.5mm (no. 7/US 7) needles and work 3 more rows. Cast/bind off loosely.

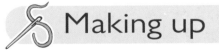 ## Making up

Do not press. Join right shoulder and neckband seam. Mark position of underarms 20[20.5:21.5:22:23.5] cm/7¾[8:8½:8¾:9¼]in down from shoulder seam on front and back. Sew in sleeves between markers. Join side and sleeve seams.

Asymmetric ribbed cardigan

This is a lovely warm and chunky cardigan, which you can wrap around yourself on a chilly day.

Easy to wear and elegantly casual, this ribbed cardigan with clever shaping and a funnel neck can be left open or fastened simply with a pin. The armholes and collar are knitted in one piece on a circular needle.

GETTING STARTED

 *Easy stitch pattern but coping with large number of stitches on circular needles for armholes and collar can be difficult*

Size:

To fit bust: 76–81[86–92:97–102]cm/30–32[34–36:38–40]in

Actual size (when stretched): 89[98:108]cm/35[38½: 42½]in

Length: 63.5[66:71]cm/25[26:28]in

Sleeve seam: 43[45.5:48.5]cm/17[18:19]in

Note: Figures in square brackets [ ] refer to larger sizes; where there is only one set of figures, it applies to all sizes

How much yarn:

20[21:22] x 50g (2oz) balls of Debbie Bliss Cashmerino Aran, approx 90m (98 yards) per ball

Needles:

Pair of 5mm (no. 6/US 8) knitting needles
5mm (no. 6/US 8) circular knitting needle, 60cm (24in) long

Additional items:

Spare knitting needles
Stitch markers
Kilt pin to fasten (optional)

Tension/gauge:

24 sts and 24 rows measure 10cm (4in) square over rib patt (slightly stretched) worked on 5mm (no. 6/US 8) needles
IT IS ESSENTIAL TO WORK TO THE STATED TENSION/GAUGE TO ACHIEVE SUCCESS

What you have to do:

Work in an irregular rib pattern. Work back, fronts and sleeves separately up to armholes. Join all stitches together on a circular needle to work armholes and collar. Work in rows on a circular needle. Work simple decreases to shape armholes.

The Yarn

Debbie Bliss Cashmerino Aran is 100% merino wool in a weight that is ideal for outer garments. It also has a crisp finish that enhances rib patterns like this.

Abbreviations:
beg = beginning;
cm = centimetre(s);
cont = continue;
inc = increase(ing);
k = knit;
p = purl; **patt** = pattern;
rem = remaining;
rep = repeat; **RS** = right
side; **st(s)** = stitch(es);
tbl = through back
of loops;
tog = together;
WS = wrong side

Instructions

BACK:

With 5mm (no. 6/US 8) needles cast on 107[117:129] sts.
1st row: (RS) (P2, k1, p1, k1) 0[1:0] times, p2, k4, p2, *k1,
p1, k1, p2, k4, p2, rep from * to last 0[5:0] sts, (k1, p1, k1,
p2) 0[1:0] times.
2nd row: (K2, p1, k1, p1) 0[1:0] times, k2, p4, k2, *p1, k1,
p1, k2, p4, k2, rep from * to last 0[5:0] sts, (p1, k1, p1, k2)
0[1:0] times.
Rep these 2 rows to form rib patt. Cont in patt until
Back measures 42[42:44.5]cm/16½[16½:17½]in from beg,
ending with a WS row.

Shape armholes:

Cast/bind off 5 sts at beg of next 2[4:2] rows. Cut off yarn
and leave rem 97[97:119] sts on a spare needle.

LEFT FRONT:

Note: Join a new ball of yarn in at the side edge when
required to keep the front edge neat.
With 5mm (no. 6/US 8) needles cast on 79[84:90] sts.
1st row: (RS) (P2, k1, p1, k1) 0[1:0] times, *p2, k4, p2, k1,
p1, k1, rep from * to last 2 sts, p1, k1.
2nd row: (P1, k1) twice, p1, k2, p4, k2, *p1, k1, p1, k2, p4,
k2, rep from * to last 0[5:0] sts, (p1, k1, p1, k2) 0[1:0] times.
Rep these 2 rows to form rib patt. Cont in patt until Left
front measures same as Back to armholes, ending with a
WS row.

Shape armhole:

Cast/bind off 5 sts at beg of next row. Patt 1 row.

2nd size only:

Cast/bind off 5 sts at beg of next row. Patt 1 row.

All sizes:

Cut off yarn and leave rem 74[74:85] sts on a
spare needle.

RIGHT FRONT:

With 5mm (no. 6/US 8) needles cast on 79[84:90] sts.
1st row: (RS) (K1, p1) twice, k1, p2, k4, p2, *k1, p1, k1, p2,
k4, p2, rep from * to last 0[5:0] sts, (k1, p1, k1, p2) 0[1:0]
times.
2nd row: (K2, p1, k1, p1) 0[1:0] times, *k2, p4, k2, p1, k1,
p1, rep from * to last 2 sts, k1, p1.
Rep these 2 rows to form rib patt. Cont in patt until Right
front measures same as Back to armholes, ending with a
RS row.

Shape armhole:

Cast/bind off 5 sts at beg of next row.

2nd size only:

Patt 1 row. Cast/bind off 5 sts at beg of next row.

All sizes:

Do not cut the yarn and leave rem 74[74:85] sts on a spare
needle.

SLEEVES:

With 5mm (no. 6/US 8) needles cast on 52[62:74] sts.
Work 4 rows in rib patt as given for Back.
Keeping patt correct and working extra sts into rib patt, inc
1 st at each end of next and every foll 6th row to 56[72:90]

sts, then at each end of every foll 4th row to 96[106:118] sts. Cont without shaping until Sleeve measures 43[45.5:48.5]cm/17[18:19]in from beg, ending with a WS row.

Shape top:
Cast/bind off 5 sts at beg of next 2[4:2] rows. Cut off yarn and leave rem 86[86:108] sts on a spare needle.

YOKE:
Note: Join a new ball of yarn in at the armhole shaping when required to keep the front edge neat.

With 5mm (no. 6/US 8) circular needle and RS of work facing, patt across 74[74:85] sts of Right front, place a marker, patt across 86[86:108] sts of first Sleeve, place a marker, patt across 97[97:119] sts of Back, place a marker, patt across 86[86:108] sts of second Sleeve, place a marker and patt across 74[74:85] sts of Left front. 417[417:505] sts
Patt 1 row, keeping rib patt correct between markers.

Shape armholes:
Next row: (RS) (Patt to within 2 sts of marker, k2tog, slip marker, k2tog tbl) 4 times, patt to end. 409[409:497] sts.
Next row: (Patt to within 2 sts of marker, p2tog tbl, slip marker, p2tog) 4 times, patt to end. 401[401: 489] sts
Rep these 2 rows, dec on every row as set, until there are 43[51:45] sts between markers for Back, 32[40:34] sts between markers for each Sleeve and 47[51:48] sts for each Front, ending with a RS row. 201[233:209] sts.
Next row: Patt to end, keeping patt correct between markers.
Next row: (RS) (Patt to within 2 sts of marker, k2tog, slip marker, k2tog tbl) 4 times, patt to end.
Rep the last 2 rows, dec on every RS row as set, until there are 33 sts between markers for Back, 22 sts between markers for each Sleeve and 42 sts between markers for each Front. 161 sts.

Collar:
Cont in rib patt without shaping until Collar measures 8cm (3in) from last dec, ending with a WS row. Cast/bind off loosely in patt.

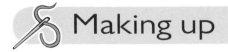 Making up

Sew in all ends. Join side seams. Join sleeve seams. Pin garment out to measurements, stretching the rib, and press according to instructions on ball band.

Cable hat with earflaps

Straightforward cable stitch makes this a great project for the novice knitter and good results will go right to your head!

Hug your head with this cosy hat in moss/seed stitch with cable panels, and the earflaps will protect your ears from biting winds.

GETTING STARTED

 *Easy stitch patterns but knitter will have to be confident with working cables and keeping pattern correct while shaping*

Size:
One size fits an average-size woman's head

How much yarn:
2 x 50g (2oz) balls of Debbie Bliss Cashmerino Aran, approx 90m (98 yards) per ball

Needles:
Pair of 4.5mm (no. 7/US 7) knitting needles
Cable needle

Additional items:
Stitch holders

Tension/gauge:
19 sts and 31 rows measure 10cm (4in) square over moss/seed st on 4.5mm (no. 7/US 7) needles
IT IS ESSENTIAL TO WORK TO THE STATED TENSION/ GAUGE TO ACHIEVE SUCCESS

What you have to do:
Start by making two earflaps in moss/seed st, leaving stitches on holders. Cast on for main part of hat, incorporating earflaps. Work main part in sections of moss/seed st separated by cable panels. Shape crown as instructed. Plait/braid cords and attach to earflaps for ties.

The Yarn
Debbie Bliss Cashmerino Aran is a luxury blend of 55% merino wool, 33% microfibre and 12% cashmere. The yarn is soft and warm, therefore ideal for a hat and it can be hand washed. There are plenty of fabulous shades to choose from.

 # Instructions

Abbreviations:

alt = alternate; **cm** = centimetre(s);
C6B = slip next 3 sts on to cable needle and hold at back of work, k3, then k3 sts from cable needle;
dec = decrease; **foll** = following; **inc** = increase; **k** = knit;
p = purl; **patt** = pattern; **rem** = remaining; **rep** = repeat;
RS = right side; **st(s)** = stitch(es); **tbl** = through back of loops; **tog** = together; **WS** = wrong side

HAT:

Earflaps: (Make 2)

With 4.5mm (no. 7/US 7) needles cast on 7 sts.
1st row: (RS) K1, (p1, k1) to end.
Rep this row to form moss/seed st. Work 1 more row. Keeping moss/seed st correct, inc 1 st at each end of next and foll 3 alt rows. 15 sts. Work 15 rows straight, ending with a WS row. Cut off yarn and leave sts on a holder.

Main part:

With 4.5mm (no. 7/US 7) needles and using 2-needle method, cast on 15 sts, then with RS facing, moss/seed st 15 sts from first earflap, turn and cast on 48 sts, turn, then with RS facing, moss/seed st 15 sts from second earflap, turn and cast on 15 sts. 108 sts.
1st row: (WS) Moss/seed st 9, (p6, moss/seed st 15) 4 times, p6, moss/seed st 9.
2nd row: Moss/seed st 9, (C6B, moss/seed st 15) 4 times, C6B, moss/seed st 9.
3rd row: As 1st row.
4th row: Moss/seed st 9, (k6, moss/seed st 15) 4 times, k6, moss/seed st 9.
5th–9th rows: Rep 3rd and 4th rows twice more, then work 3rd row again.
The 2nd–9th rows form cable patt. Rep them 3 times more, then work 6 more rows in patt, ending with a WS row.

Shape crown:

1st dec row: (RS) Moss/seed st 7, work 2tog tbl, (k6, work 2tog, moss/seed st 11, work 2tog tbl) 4 times, k6, work 2tog, moss/seed st 7. 98 sts.
Patt 3 rows straight as set (the first RS row is a cable row).
2nd dec row: Moss/seed st 6, work 2tog tbl, (k6, work 2tog, moss/seed st 9, work 2tog tbl) 4 times, k6, work 2tog, moss/seed st 6. 88 sts.
Patt 3 rows straight as set. Cont in this way, dec 10 sts on

next and every foll alt row until 48 sts rem.
Patt 1 row.
Next row: K1, p2tog tbl, (k6, p3tog) 4 times, k6, p2tog, k1. 38 sts.
Next row: (WS) K2, (p6, k1) 5 times, k1.
Next row: K1, p1, (C6B, p1) 5 times, k1.
Next row: K2, *(p3tog) twice, k1*, rep from * to * 4 times more, k1. 18 sts.
Cut off yarn, thread through rem sts, draw up and fasten off securely.

✂ Making up

Join back seam. Cut six 80cm (32in) long strands of yarn. Double over and attach folded end to centre of cast-on edge of one earflap. Plait/braid a cord, then knot ends to form a tassel. Repeat for second earflap.

HOW TO
ATTACH CORDS

Decorative plaited/braided cords are attached to each earflap of this cable hat.

1 For one earflap, cut six lengths of yarn each measuring 80cm (32in).

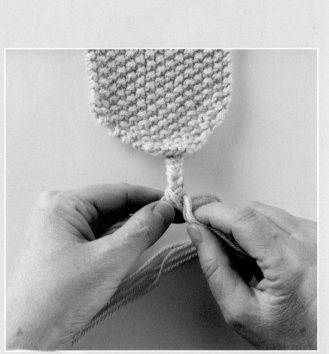

3 Divide the lengths of yarn into three groups of four strands. Plait/braid the groups of yarn, keeping the strands as flat as possible.

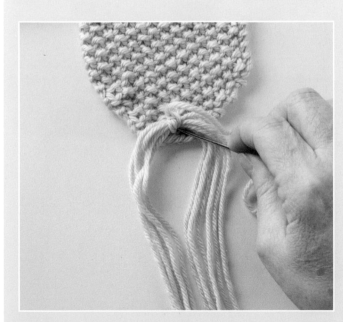

2 Place the lengths together and fold over to find the mid-point. Using a blunt-ended needle, sew the strands to the wrong side of the flap at the mid-point. Secure the yarn neatly and cut off.

4 Plait/braid to within 7cm (2¾in) of the ends of the yarn and then tie with a single knot. Trim the ends of the yarn if necessary. Repeat with the second earflap.

Simple Fair Isle socks

Supercool colours and a traditional pattern are a winning combination for these Fair Isle favourites.

These attractive patterned socks are knitted in the round for a smooth, seamless finish. They include a simplified way of working the heel without the complications that are more usual in this traditional style of sock.

The Yarn

King Cole Zig Zag 4-ply contains 50% superwash wool and 50% nylon, which is an ideal combination for items that need to be washed again and again without losing their shape. There are plenty of fabulous colours including some variegated ones to choose from for interesting Fair Isle patterns.

GETTING STARTED

Simple design but take care with making up for a neat finish

Size:

To fit shoe sizes 4–6 (6½–8½)

Foot length: *21.5cm (8½in)*

Leg length (with top rolled down): *25cm (10in)*

How much yarn:

1 x 100g (3½oz) balls of King Cole Zig Zag 4-ply, approx 448m (493 yards) per ball, in each of colours A and B

Needles:

Set of 3.25mm (no. 10/US 3) double-pointed needles

Additional items:

Length of smooth yarn in contrast colour

Tension/gauge:

34 sts and 39 rows measure 10cm (4in) square over Fair Isle patt on 3.25mm (no. 10/US 3) needles

IT IS ESSENTIAL TO WORK TO THE STATED TENSION/ GAUGE TO ACHIEVE SUCCESS

What you have to do:

Work in rounds of stocking/stockinette stitch (knit every round). Follow chart to work Fair Isle pattern. Strand or weave colour not in use across back of work. Graft toe stitches together for a seamless join. After working leg, work stitches for heel in a contrast yarn. After finishing, remove contrast yarn, pick up heel stitches and shape as given for toe.

Instructions

Abbreviations:

cm = centimetre(s); **cont** = continue;
k = knit; **patt** = pattern;
psso = pass slipped stitch over;
RS = right side; **sl** = slip; **st(s)** = stitch(es);
tog = together; **WS** = wrong side

Note: You can use a set of 4 or a set
of 5 double-pointed needles. If using
4 needles, cast on 24 sts on to each of
3 needles to work main part of sock, then
for toe and heel, rearrange the sts so that
half are on one needle and a quarter are
on each of the other two needles. If using
5 needles, cast on 18 sts on to each of 4
needles. There is no need to rearrange sts
for toe and heel.

LEFT SOCK:

Leg:

With A, cast on 72 sts and arrange as given
in Note. Bring first and last needles together
to join in a round. Cont in A, k 24 rounds.
Join in B. Cont in patt from chart, reading
each round from right to left, k each round
and strand or weave yarn not in use loosely across
WS of work. Work 70 rounds. ******

Heel opening round: Patt 37 sts, cut off A and B
leaving 10cm (4in)-long ends. Using separate smooth
yarn in a contrast colour, k35.

Foot:

Join in A and B and cont in patt over all sts for 46
rounds. Cut off B. Cont in A only, k 3 rounds.

Shape toe:

1st round: (K1, k2tog, k31, sl 1, k1, psso) twice.
68 sts.
K 1 round.
3rd round: (K1, k2tog, k29, sl 1, k1, psso) twice.
64 sts.
K 1 round.
5th round: (K1, k2tog, k27, sl 1, k1, psso) twice.
60 sts.
K 1 round.
7th round: (K1, k2tog, k25, sl 1, k1, psso) twice.
56 sts.

K 1 round.
9th round: (K1, k2tog, k23, sl 1, k1, psso) twice. 52 sts.
K 1 round.
11th round: (K1, k2tog, k21, sl 1, k1, psso) twice. 48 sts.
K 1 round.
13th round: (K1, k2tog, k19, sl 1, k1, psso) twice. 44 sts.
14th round: (K1, k2tog, k17, sl 1, k1, psso) twice. 40
sts.
15th round: (K1, k2tog, k15, sl 1, k1, psso) twice. 36 sts.
Arrange 18 sts on each of 2 needles and graft sts tog.

Heel:

With RS facing, undo contrast yarn, placing 35 sts below
and 35 loops at base of sts above on needles.
1st round: With A, pick up and k one st from row-end
before sts, k35 sts, pick up and k one st from row-end
after sts, k35 loops from base of sts. 72 sts.
K 2 more rounds. Complete as given for toe shaping.
Darn in ends. Roll down top for 2cm (¾in).

RIGHT SOCK:

Work as given for Left sock to **.

Heel opening round: Patt 1 st, cut off A and B leaving 10cm (4in)-long ends. Using separate smooth yarn in a contrast colour, k35, rejoin A and B and patt 36 sts. Complete as given for Left sock.

Sweater with Fair Isle bands

A simple shape combined with bands of intarsia pattern is the ideal way to practise your knitting skills.

A drop-shoulder style with rolled edges, this boxy-shape sweater has horizontal bands of distinctive Fair Isle patterns in a second colour across the back and front.

GETTING STARTED

 *Sweater requires minimum of shaping but working Fair Isle pattern requires practise*

Size:

To fit bust: *81–86[91–97:102–107]cm/32–34[36–38:40–42]in*

Actual bust size: *93[105:117]cm/36½[41½:46]in*

Length: *55[58:60]cm/21½[23:23¾]in*

Sleeve seam: *43[44:46]cm/17[17½:18]in*

Note: *Figures in square brackets [ ] refer to larger sizes; where there is only one set of figures, it applies to all sizes*

How much yarn:

14[15:16] x 50g (2oz) balls of Debbie Bliss Cotton DK, approx 84m (92 yards) per ball, in main colour M

1[2:2] balls in contrast colour C

Needles:

Pair of 3.75mm (no. 9/US 5) knitting needles

Pair of 4mm (no. 8/US 6) knitting needles

Pair of 4.5mm (no. 7/US 7) knitting needles

3.75mm (no. 9/US 5) circular knitting needle for collar

Tension/gauge:

20 sts and 28 rows measure 10cm (4in) square over st st on 4mm (no. 8/US 6) needles; 7-row patt measures 3cm (1⅛in) on 4.5mm (no. 7/US 7) needles

IT IS ESSENTIAL TO WORK TO THE STATED TENSION/GAUGE TO ACHIEVE SUCCESS

What you have to do:

Work in stocking/stockinette stitch with main colour. At intervals join in contrast colour and knit bands of Fair Isle pattern, stranding yarn not in use across wrong side of work. Use simple shaping for front neckline and sleeves. Pick up stitches around neckline with circular needle for collar and work in rounds of stocking/stockinette stitch.

The Yarn

Debbie Bliss Cotton DK is 100% cotton. With a slight twist and matt finish, it produces good stitch definition and is available in plenty of colourful shades for interesting colour work. The yarn is also machine washable at a low temperature.

Abbreviations:

beg = beginning;
cm = centimetre(s);
cont = continue;
foll = follow(s)(ing);
inc = increase; **k** = knit;
p = purl; **patt** = pattern;
psso = pass slipped stitch over;
rem = remain;
rep = repeat;
RS = right side;
sl = slip; **st(s)** = stitch(es);
st st = stocking/
stockinette stitch;
tog = together;
WS = wrong side

Instructions

BACK:

With 3.75mm (no. 9/US 5) needles and M, cast on 93[105:117] sts. *Beg with a k row, work 4 rows in st st. Change to 4mm (no. 8/US 6) needles. Work 12 rows more in st st. Change to 4.5mm (no. 7/US 7) needles. Cont in patt, stranding yarn loosely across WS of work, as foll:

1st row: (RS) K4 M, (1 C, 5 M) to last 5 sts, 1 C, 4 M.
2nd row: P3 M, (1 C, 1 M, 1 C, 3 M, 3 C, 3 M) to last 6 sts, 1 C, 1 M, 1 C, 3 M.
3rd row: K2 M, (1 C, 1 M, 1 C, 1 M, 1 C, 1 M, 2 C, 1 M, 2 C, 1 M) to last 7 sts, 1 C, 1 M, 1 C, 1 M, 1 C, 2 M.
4th row: P1 M, (1 C, 1 M, 3 C, 1 M, 2 C, 3 M, 1 C) to last 8 sts, 1 C, 1 M, 3 C, 1 M, 1 C, 1 M.
5th row: As 3rd row.
6th row: As 2nd row.
7th row: As 1st row. *
Change to 4mm (no. 8/US 6) needles. Beg with a p row, work 43[45:47] rows st st in M. Rep last 50[52:54] rows once more. Change to 4.5mm (no. 7/US 7) needles. Patt 7 rows as before.**
Change to 4mm (no. 8/US 6) needles. Cont in M only and beg with a p row, work 29 [31:33] rows in st st.

Shape shoulders:

Next row: Cast/bind off 24[28:32] sts, k until there are 45[49:53] sts on right-hand needle, cast/bind off rem 24[28:32] sts. Cut off yarn and leave centre 45[49:53] sts on a holder.

FRONT:

Work as given for Back to **.

COLLAR:

Join shoulder seams.

With 3.75mm (no. 9/US 5) circular needle and M, pick up and k 13[15:17] sts down left front neck, k across 31[33:35] front neck sts from holder, pick up and k 13[15:17] sts up right front neck and k across 45[49:53] back neck sts from holder. 102[112:122] sts. Work 14[16:18] rounds in st st (every round k).

Cast/bind off.

Making up

Press according to instructions on ball band. Sew in sleeves approximately 19[20:22]cm/7½[8:8½]in below shoulders. Join side and sleeve seams, reversing seams for 4 rows from cast-on edges to allow for roll.

Change to 4mm (no. 8/US 6) needles. Cont in M only and beg with a p row, work 13 rows in st st.

Shape neck:

Next row: (RS) K31[36:41], turn and leave rem sts on a holder.

Next row: P to end.

Next row: K to last 3 sts, k2tog, k1.

Rep last 2 rows 6[7:8] times more. 24[28:32] sts.

P 1 row. Cast/bind off.

Return to sts a base of neck, sl centre 31[33:35] sts on to a holder, with RS facing join yarn to rem sts and k to end.

Next row: P to end.

Next row: K1, sl 1, k1, psso, k to end.

Complete to match first side of neck.

SLEEVES:

With 3.75mm (no. 9/US 5) needles and M, cast on 57 sts. Work as given for Back from * to *.

Change to 4mm (no. 8/US 6) needles. Cont in M only, p 1 row then inc 1 st at each end of next and every foll 8th[8th:6th] row until there are 77[81:87] sts. Work 23[11:19] rows straight, ending with a p row. Cast/bind off.

Cushion with petals

Worked in jewel-bright colours, this cushion/pillow cover makes a striking note on a sofa or bed.

Instantly jazz up this simple cushion/pillow by stitching on a scattering of colourful knitted petals.

GETTING STARTED

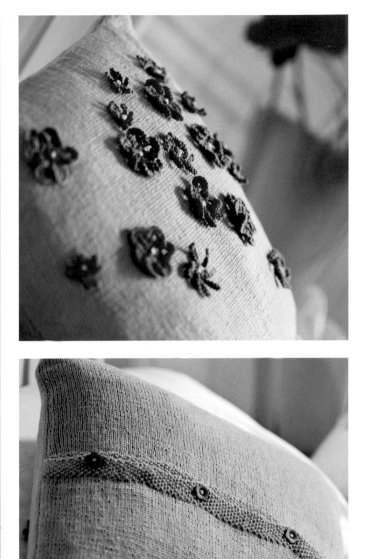

Cushion/pillow cover is easy stocking/ stockinette stitch but keep the stitches even for a good finished effect

Size:
Cushion/pillow is 46cm x 46cm (18in x 18in)

How much yarn:
2 x 100g (3½oz) balls of Patons 100% Cotton 4-ply, approx 330m (361 yards) per ball, in main colour A
1 ball in each of four contrast colours B, C, D and E

Needles:
Pair of 3.25mm (no. 10/US 3) knitting needles

Additional items:
4 buttons
46cm (18in) square cushion pad/pillow form

Tension/gauge:
28 sts and 36 rows measure 10cm (4in) square over st st on 3.25mm (no. 10/US 3) needles
IT IS ESSENTIAL TO WORK TO THE STATED TENSION/GAUGE TO ACHIEVE SUCCESS

What you have to do:
Work cushion/pillow front in stocking/stockinette stitch. Work backs in stocking/stockinette stitch with moss/seed stitch button and buttonhole bands. Work a selection of flowers in a variety of colours. Sew flowers to cushion/pillow front in a random pattern. Embroider French knots in flower centres.

The Yarn
Patons 100% cotton 4-ply is a pure cotton yarn that has a slight twist and a subtle sheen. There are plenty of pastel, bright and contemporary subtle shades to create any colourway required.

Abbreviations:

beg = beginning;
cm = centimetre(s);
cont = continue;
foll = follow(s)(ing);
k = knit; **p** = purl;
patt = pattern;
rem = remain(ing);
rep = repeat;
RS = right side;
sl = slip;
st(s) = stitch(es);
st st = stocking/
stockinette stitch;
tbl = through back of loop;
tog = together;
WS = wrong side;
yo = yarn over or round
needle to make
a stitch

Instructions

FRONT:

With A, cast on 128 sts. Beg with a
k row, cont in st st until work measures 46cm (18in) from
beg, ending with a p row. Cast/bind off.

BACK:
Top half:

With A, cast on 128 sts. Beg with a k row, cont in st st until
work measures 21.5cm (8½in) from beg, ending with a p
row.
Next row: (K1, p1) to end.
Next row: (P1, k1) to end.
Rep last 2 rows once more to form moss/seed st.
Buttonhole row: (RS) Patt 18 sts, (yo, work 2tog, patt
28 sts) 3 times, yo, work 2tog, patt 18 sts.
Work 5 more rows in moss/seed st. Cast/bind off in patt.

Bottom half:

With A, cast on 128 sts. Beg with a k row, cont in st st until
work measures 21.5cm (8½in) from beg, ending with a
p row.
Next row: (K1, p1) to end.
Next row: (P1, k1) to end.

Rep last 2 rows 4 times more to form moss/seed st. Cast/
bind off in patt.

FLOWERS:

Petal flower: (Make 4 with B as outer colour and centre
in C; make another 4 with C as outer colour and centre in
D)
With outer colour, cast on 68 sts. P 1 row.
Next row: K2, (k1, sl this st back on to left needle, pass
next 8 sts over top of this st and off needle, (yo) twice to
make 2 sts, k slipped st again, k2) to end. 32 sts.
Next row: P1, (p2tog, p1, p1 tbl, p1) to last st,
p1. 26 sts. Change to centre colour.
Next row: (K2tog) to end. 13 sts. P 1 row.
Next row: K1, (k2tog) to end. 7 sts.
Cut off yarn, thread through rem sts, draw up tightly and
sew row ends tog to form a flower.
Tufted flower: small[medium] (Make 3 small flowers
in C and 4 in D; make 2 medium flowers in each of C
and D)
With required colour, make a slip knot and place on
needle.

Next row: (Cast on 5[8] sts to give 6[9] sts on needle, Cast/bind off 5[8] sts, sl rem st back on to left needle) 7 times.

Fasten off rem st. Thread yarn through all slipped sts, gather up and fasten off to form flower.

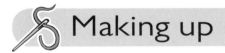 ## Making up

Press cushion/pillow front and backs according to directions on ball band. Using photograph (above left) as a guide, sew flowers to front in a random formation. Embroider a French knot with E in centre of all flowers. With RS facing, sew cushion/pillow backs to front, overlapping button band over buttonhole band in centre. Turn RS out. Sew on buttons to correspond with buttonholes.

Embroidered circles cardigan

Embellish this stylish cardigan with embroidered circles along the hem.

Fastened with a single large button, this stocking/stockinette stitch cardigan has a neat rever collar in moss/seed stitch and embroidered circles.

GETTING STARTED

Basic fabric but with lots of shaping and requires neat knitting for good results

Size:

To fit bust: *81–86[91–97:102–107]cm/32–34[36–38:40–42]in*

Actual size: *90[101:112]cm/35½[39¾:44]in*

Length: *56[57.5:59]cm/22[22½:23¼]in*

Sleeve seam: *45[46:46.5]cm/17¾[18:18½]in*

Note: *Figures in square brackets [ ] refer to larger sizes; where there is only one set of figures, it applies to all sizes*

How much yarn:

11[12:12] x 50g (2oz) balls of Debbie Bliss Rialto Aran, approx 80m (87 yards) per ball, in main colour
1 ball in each of two contrasting colours for embroidery

Needles:

Pair of 4mm (no. 8/US 6) knitting needles
Pair of 5mm (no. 6/US 8) knitting needles
Additional items:
1 large button
Stitch holders and safety pins
Tapestry needle for embroidery

Tension/gauge:

18 sts and 24 rows measure 10cm (4in) square over st st on 5mm (no. 6/US 8) needles
IT IS ESSENTIAL TO WORK TO THE STATED TENSION/ GAUGE TO ACHIEVE SUCCESS

What you have to do:

Work lower borders, front bands and collar in moss/ seed stitch. Work main fabric in stocking/stockinette stitch. Use fashioned shaping for armhole and neck edges. Work collar and shape lapels as instructed. Embroider circles using chain stitch.

The Yarn

Debbie Bliss Rialto Aran contains 100% merino wool. This luxury yarn gives good stitch definition for stocking/stockinette stitch fabrics and it can be washed at a low temperature. There are plenty of fashionable shades to choose from.

Abbreviations:

alt = alternate;
beg = beginning;
cm = centimetre(s);
cont = continue;
dec = decrease(ing);
foll = follow(s)(ing);
inc = increase(ing);
k = knit;
m l = make one stitch by picking up strand lying between needles and working into back of it;
p = purl;
psso = pass slipped stitch over;
rem = remain(ing);
rep = repeat;
RS = right side; **sl** = slip;
st(s) = stitch(es);
st st = stocking/stockinette stitch;
tog = together;
WS = wrong side

Instructions

BACK:

With 4mm (no. 8/US 6) needles cast on 83[93:103] sts.

1st row: (RS) K1, (p1, k1) to end. Rep this row to form moss/seed st. Work 7 more rows in moss/seed st, ending with a WS row. Change to 5mm (no. 6/US 8) needles. Beg with a k row, work 82[84:86] rows in st st, ending with a WS row.

Shape armholes:

Cast/bind off 3[4:5] sts at beg of next 2 rows. 77[85:93] sts.

Next row: K3, sl 1, k1, psso, k to last 5 sts, k2tog, k3. Beg with a p row, work 3 rows in st st. Rep last 4 rows 6[7:8] times more, then work dec row again. 61[67:73] sts. Beg with a p row, work 15[13:11] rows straight, ending with a WS row.

Shape shoulders:

Next row: Cast/bind off 13[15:17] sts, k until there are 35[37:39] sts on right-hand needle, Cast/bind off rem 13[15:17] sts.

Leave rem 35[37:39] sts on a holder.

LEFT FRONT:

With 4mm (no. 8/US 6) needles cast on 43[47:53] sts. Work 8 rows in moss/seed st as given for Back.

Change to 5mm (no. 6/US 8) needles.

Next row: (RS) Inc in first st for 2nd size only, k to last 6 sts, inc in next st, turn and leave rem 5 sts on a safety-pin for front band. 39[44:49] sts.

Beg with a p row, work 63[65:67] rows in st st, ending with a WS row.

Shape neck:

Next row: K to last 5 sts, k2tog, k3. Beg with a p row, work 3 rows in st st. Rep last 4 rows 3 times more, then work dec row again. 34[39:44] sts. P 1 row, so ending at armhole edge.

Shape armhole:

Cast/bind off 3[4:5] sts at beg of next row. P 1 row.

Next row:K3, sl 1, k1, psso, k to last 5 sts, k2tog, k3.

Beg with a p row, work 3 rows in st st. Rep last 4 rows 6[7:8] times more, then work dec row again. 15[17:19] sts. Keeping armhole edge straight, cont to dec at neck edge as set on 2 foll 4th rows. 13[15:17] sts. Work 7[5:3] rows straight, ending with a WS row. Cast/bind off.

RIGHT FRONT:

With 4mm (no. 8/US 6) needles cast on 43[47:53] sts. Work 8 rows in moss/seed st as given for Back.

Next row: (RS) Moss/seed st 4, inc in next st and sl these 6 sts on to a safety pin, change to 5mm (no. 6/US 8) needles, cast on 1 st, k to end, inc in last st for 2nd size only. 39[44:49] sts. Beg with a p row, work 63[65:67] rows in st st, ending with a WS row.

Shape neck:

Next row: K3, sl 1, k1, psso, k to end.

Beg with a p row, work 3 rows in st st. Rep last 4 rows 3 times more, then work dec row again. 34[39:44] sts. P 1 row and k 1 row, so ending at armhole edge.

Shape armhole:

Cast/bind off 3[4:5] sts at beg of next row.
Complete as given for Left front from * to end.

SLEEVES: (Make 2)

With 4mm (no. 8/US 6) needles cast on 37[41:45] sts. Work 8 rows in moss/seed st as given for Back. Change to 5mm (no. 6/US 8) needles.

Next row: K3, m1, k to last 3 sts, m1, k3.

Beg with a p row, work 7 rows in st st. Rep last 8 rows 11 times more, then work inc row again. 63[67:71] sts. Work 5[7:9] rows straight, ending with a WS row.

Shape top:

Cast/bind off 3[4:5] sts at beg of next 2 rows. Dec 1 st at each end of next and 1[3:5] foll alt rows, ending with a WS row. 53[51:49] sts. Now dec 1 st at each end of every row until 17[19:21] sts rem. Cast/bind off.

LEFT FRONT BAND:

With 4mm (no. 8/US 6) needles cast on 1 st, then with RS facing work in moss/seed st across 5 sts from safety-pin. 6 sts.

Next row: (WS) (K1, p1) to end.

Next row: (P1, k1) to end.

Cont in moss/seed st as set until band, when slightly stretched, fits up front edge to beg of neck shaping. Cast/bind off in moss/seed st.

RIGHT FRONT BAND:

With WS of work facing, join yarn to inside edge of 6 sts on safety-pin, (p1, k1) to end.

Next row: (K1, p1) to end.

Cont in moss/seed st as set until band, when slightly stretched, fits up front edge to beg of neck shaping. Cast/bind off in moss/seed st.

COLLAR:

With 4mm (no. 8/US 6) needles cast on 3 sts, then with RS facing work across 35[37:39] back neck sts on holder as foll: (k1, p1) to last st, inc in last st, turn. 39[41:43] sts. Keeping moss/seed st correct, cont in this way, casting on 3 sts at beg of every row and inc 1 st at end of every row, until there are 107[109:111] sts, ending with a WS row.

Work lapels:

Next row: Cast on 3 sts and moss/seed st these 3 sts, moss/seed st 23, turn and cont on these 26 sts for right lapel as foll:

Next row: Moss/seed st to last st, inc in last st.

Cont as set, work 4 more rows, ending with a WS row. 35 sts. Work 5 rows straight. Cast/bind off loosely in moss/seed st.

With RS facing, rejoin yarn to rem 84[86:88] sts, work to last 23 sts, turn and work 12 more rows in moss/seed st on these 61[63:65] sts from back collar. Cast/bind off loosely in moss/seed st. With RS facing, rejoin yarn to rem 23 sts for left lapel, work to last st, inc in last st.

Next row: Cast on 3 sts, work to end. 27 sts.

Cont as set, work 4 rows more, ending with a WS row. 35 sts. Work 5 rows straight. Cast/bind off loosely in moss/seed st.

✍ Making up

Press according to directions on ball band, avoiding moss/seed st sections.

Using the photograph (left) as a guide and two contrast colours, embroider circles at random all around lower edges of back and fronts above moss/seed st border. Work 5 or 6 chain sts for small circles approximately 1cm–2cm (½in–¾in) diameter, and up to 20 sts for larger circles of 4cm (1½in) diameter. Work another circle of chain sts inside some circles in either the same colour or the other colour.

Join shoulder seams. Sew on front bands, ending at beg of neck shaping. Sew collar to neck edge, joining row-ends of straight rows to cast/bound-off sts of bands and leaving an opening where right lapel meets front band for buttonhole. Sew in sleeves. Join side and sleeve seams. Sew on button.

Bobble bolster cushion

Put your feet up and lean back on this colourful bolster adorned with bobbles.

This traditional bolster, with gathered ends trimmed with a button and a crochet edging, is knitted in a lively colourway with stripes and multi-coloured bobbles.

The Yarn

Debbie Bliss Prima is a double knitting (light worsted) weight yarn containing 80% bamboo and 20% merino wool. It produces a soft fabric with clear stitch definition and there are plenty of colours for interesting colour work. We also used Debbie Bliss Cashmerino DK in bright pink to create this particular colour combination.

GETTING STARTED

Mainly straightforward stocking/ stockinette stitch but working individual coloured bobbles might need some practise

Size:
Bolster is 46cm long x 20cm in diameter (18in x 8in)

How much yarn:
2 x 50g (2oz) balls of Debbie Bliss Prima, approx 106m (116 yards) per ball, in each of three colours A, B and C
1 ball in colour D
1 x 50g (2oz) ball of Debbie Bliss Cashmerino DK, approx 110m (120 yards) per ball, in colour E

Needles:
Pair of 3.25mm (no. 10/US 3) knitting needles
Pair of 4mm (no. 8/US 6) knitting needles

Additional items:
4.00mm (no. 8/US 6) crochet hook
35cm (14in) zip fastener
2 x 38mm buttons for covering
46cm x 20cm diameter (18in x 8in) bolster cushion pad/pillow form

Tension/gauge:
22 sts and 30 rows measure 10cm (4in) square over st st on 4mm (no. 8/US 6) needles
IT IS ESSENTIAL TO WORK TO THE STATED TENSION/GAUGE TO ACHIEVE SUCCESS

What you have to do:
Work main part of bolster in stocking/stockinette stitch with stripes and coloured bobbles. Add crochet edging trim to ends of main part. Create circular ends of bolster in stocking/stockinette stitch with turning rows. Knit cover for buttons and sew to centre of bolster ends. Sew zip fastener into seam for easy removal of cushion pad/pillow form.

Instructions

Abbreviations:

beg = beginning;
cm = centimetre(s);
cont = continue;
dc = double crochet (US
sc = single crochet);
foll = following;
inc = increase(ing);
k = knit;
p = purl; **rep** = repeat;
RS = right side; **sl** = slip;
ss = slip stitch (crochet);
st(s) = stitch(es);
st st = stocking/
stockinette stitch;
tbl = through back of loop;
tog = together; **tr** = treble
(US **dc** = double crochet)

Make bobble:

Join in required colour. Work into front and back of next st until there are 5 sts, turn. Beg with a p row, work 4 rows st st on these 5 sts.
Next row: P2tog, p1, p2tog. 3 sts.
Next row: With base colour, k3tog, then cont along row according to instructions.

BOLSTER MAIN PIECE:

With 4mm (no. 8/US 6) needles and D, cast on 152 sts. Beg with a k row, work 4 rows in st st. Cont in st st and stripes of 4 rows each C and E.
Change to A and work 8 rows.

Place bobbles:

Next row: (RS) With A, k20, mb in C, k21, mb in D, k21, mb in E, k21, mb in B, k21, mb in C, k21, mb in D, k21. Beg with a p row, work 11 rows in st st.
Next row: (RS) With A, k9, mb in E, k21, mb in B, k21, mb in C, k21, mb in D, k21, mb in E, k21, mb in B, k21, mb in C, k10. Beg with a p row, work 11 rows in st st.
Next row: (RS) With A, k20, mb in D, k21, mb in E, k21, mb in B, k21, mb in C, k21, mb in D, k21, mb in E, k21. Beg with a p row, work 11 rows in st st.
Next row: (RS) With A, k9, mb in B, k21, mb in C, k21,

mb in D, k21, mb in E, k21, mb in B, k21, mb in C, k21, mb in D, k10. Beg with a p row, work 7 rows in st st.
Cont in st st and stripes of 4 rows each D, E and C. Change to B and work 8 rows.

Place bobbles:

Next row: (RS) With B, k20, mb in C, k21, mb in D, k21, mb in E, k21, mb in A, k21, mb in C, k21, mb in D, k21. Beg with a p row, work 11 rows in st st.
Next row: (RS) With B, k9, mb in E, k21, mb in A, k21, mb in C, k21, mb in D, k21, mb in E, k21, mb in A, k21, mb in C, k10. Beg with a p row, work 11 rows in st st.
Next row: (RS) With B, k20, mb in D, k21, mb in E, k21, mb in A, k21, mb in C, k21, mb in D, k21, mb in E, k21. Beg with a p row, work 11 rows in st st.
Next row: (RS) With B, k9, mb in A, k21, mb in C, k21, mb in D, k21, mb in E, k21, mb in A, k21, mb in C, k21, mb in D, k10. Beg with a p row, work 7 rows in st st.
Cont in st st and stripes of 4 rows each C, E and D. Cast/bind off.

Scallop edging:

With 4mm (no. 8/US 6) crochet hook, E and RS of work facing, work 151dc (US sc) along cast-on edge.
Next row: Ss in first dc (US sc), (miss 2dc (US sc), 5tr (US dc) in next dc (US sc), miss 2dc (US sc), ss in next dc (US

sc)) to end. Fasten off.
Rep scallop edging along cast/bound-off edge.

END PIECE: (Make 2)
With 4mm (no. 8/US 6) needles and C, cast on 21 sts.
K 1 row and p 1 row.
*Next 2 rows: K20, turn; sl 1, p to end.
Next 2 rows: K19, turn; sl 1, p to end.
Cont in this way until foll 2 rows have been worked 'K5, turn; sl 1, p to end.'
Next row: K4, (pick up front loop of st below sl st and place on left-hand needle, k it tog tbl with next sl st) 16 times, k1. P 1 row.*
Rep from * to * 5 times more. Cast/bind off.

BUTTON COVER: (Make 2)
With 3.25mm (no. 10/US 3) needles and E, cast on 11 sts.
Next row: K to end.
Next row: P to end.
Next row: K to end, inc in first and last sts.
Next row: P to end.
Rep last 2 rows twice more. 17 sts. Beg with a k row, work 4 rows in st st.

Next row: K2tog, k to last 2 sts, k2tog.
Next row: P to end.
Rep last 2 rows twice more. 11 sts. Cast/bind off.

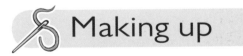

Making up

Sew cast-on and cast/bound-off edges of each end piece tog. Gather up centre of each one. Cover buttons according to manufacturer's instructions and sew to centre of end pieces.
Join side edges of main piece for approximately 6cm (2½in) from each end. Sew zip fastener into opening. Sew in end pieces to each end of open tube formed by main piece, taking care not to catch in scallop edging. Insert cushion pad/pillow form and close zip fastener.

Long-line lace cardigan

As lace patterns go, this one is easy to knit and the result is a picture-perfect cardigan.

This elegant long-line lacy cardigan with moss/seed stitch bands has a small curved collar and is fitted through the bodice with ribbing.

The Yarn

Sublime Extra Fine Merino Wool DK contains 100% merino wool. It is a luxuriously smooth yarn giving clear stitch definition and can be machine washed at a low temperature. There are plenty of beautiful subtle colours to choose from.

GETTING STARTED

Lace patterns can be difficult to keep correct when shaping, but this one is fairly easy

Size:

To fit bust: 81–86[91–97:102–107]cm/32–34 [36–38:40–42]in

Actual size: 88[102.5:110]cm/34½[40½:43¼]in

Length: 66.5[68.5:70.5]cm/26[27:27¾]in

Sleeve seam: 46[46:47]cm/18[18:18½]in

Note: Figures in square brackets [ ] refer to larger sizes; where there is only one set of figures, it applies to all sizes

How much yarn:

12[13:14] x 50g (2oz) balls of Sublime Extra Fine Merino Wool DK, approx 116m (127 yards) per ball

Needles:

Pair of 3.25mm (no. 10/US 3) knitting needles

Pair of 4mm (no. 8/US 6) knitting needles

Additional items:

Stitch holder, 8 buttons

Tension/gauge:

22 sts and 28 rows measure 10cm (4in) square over lace patt on 4mm (no. 8/US 6) needles

IT IS ESSENTIAL TO WORK TO THE STATED TENSION/GAUGE TO ACHIEVE SUCCESS

What you have to do:

Work lower edge, cuffs, front bands and collar in moss/seed stitch. Work lacy pattern for main fabric as instructed. Draw in bodice with band of single (k1, p1) rib. Make simple 'yarn-over' buttonholes. Pick up stitches around neckline for collar.

 ## Instructions

BACK:

With 3.25mm (no. 10/US 3) needles cast on 105[121: 129] sts.

1st row: (RS) K1, *p1, k1, rep from * to end.

Rep this row to form moss/seed st, work 6 more rows in moss/seed st.

Change to 4mm (no. 8/US 6) needles. Cont in lace patt as foll:

1st row: (WS) P to end.

2nd row: K1, *k2tog, yo, k3, yo, sl 1, k1, psso, k1, rep from * to end.

3rd row: P to end.

4th row: K3, *yo, sl 1, k2tog, psso, yo, k5, rep from * ending last rep with k3.

These 4 rows form lace patt. Cont in patt until Back measures 31cm (12¼in) from beg, ending with a WS row. Change to 3.25mm (no. 10/US 3) needles.

1st row: (RS) K2, *p1, k1, rep from * to last st, k1.

2nd row: K1, *p1, k1, rep from * to end.

Abbreviations:
alt = alternate;
beg = beginning;
cm = centimetre(s);
cont = continue;
dec = decrease(ing);
foll = follow(s)(ing);
inc = increase(ing);
k = knit; **p** = purl;
patt = pattern;
psso = pass slipped stitch over;
rem = remain(ing);
rep = repeat;
RS = right side; **sl** = slip;
st(s) = stitch(es);
tog = together;
WS = wrong side;
yo = yarn over or round needle to make a stitch

Cont in rib as set until Back measures 39cm (15½in) from beg, ending with a WS row.

Dec row: Rib 9[10:7], *work 2tog, rib 10[12:14], rep from * 6 times more, work 2tog, rib 10[11:8]. 97[113:121] sts. Change to 4mm (no. 8/US 6) needles. Beg with a 1st row, cont in lace patt until Back measures 47cm (18½in) from beg, ending with a WS row.

Shape armholes:
Cast/bind off 6 sts at beg of next 2 rows. Dec 1 st at each end of next 6 rows, then at each end of every foll alt row until 65[81:89] sts rem. Work straight until armholes measure 18[20:22]cm/7[7¾:8½]in, ending with a WS row.

Shape back neck:
Next row: Patt 18[25:28] sts, turn and complete this side of neck first. Patt 4 rows, dec 1 st at neck edge on every row. Cast/bind off rem 14[21:24] sts. With RS of work facing, sl centre 29[31:33] sts on to a holder, rejoin yarn to next st and patt to end. Complete as given for first side of neck.

LEFT FRONT:
With 3.25mm (no. 10/US 3) needles cast on 49[57:61] sts. Work 7 rows in moss/seed st as given for Back.
Change to 4mm (no. 8/US 6) needles. Cont in lace patt as foll:

1st and 2nd sizes only:
Work as given for Back.

3rd size only:
1st row: (WS) P to end.
2nd row: K1, *k2tog, yo, k3, yo, sl 1, k1, psso, k1, rep from * to last 4 sts, k2tog, yo, k2.

3rd row: P to end.
4th row: K3, *yo, sl 1, k2tog, psso, yo, k5, rep from * to last 2 sts, yo, sl 1, k1, psso.

** All sizes:
Cont in patt until Front measures 31cm (12¼in) from beg, ending with a WS row. Change to 3.25mm (no. 10/US 3) needles.

1st row: (RS) K2, *p1, k1, rep from * to last st, k1.
2nd row: K1, *p1, k1, rep from * to end.
Cont in rib as set until Front measures 39cm (15½in) from beg, ending with a WS row.

Dec row: Rib 7[8:7], *work 2 tog, rib 9[11:13], rep from * twice more, work 2 tog, rib 7[8:7]. 45[53:57] sts.
Change to 4mm (no. 8/US 6) needles. Beg with 1st row, cont in lace patt as foll: ******

1st and 2nd sizes only:
1st row: (WS) P to end.
2nd row: K1, *k2tog, yo, k3, yo, sl 1, k1, psso, k1, rep from * to last 4 sts, k2tog, yo, k2.

3rd row: P to end.
4th row: K3, *yo, sl 1, k2tog, psso, yo, k5, rep from * to last 2 sts, yo, sl 1, k1, psso.

3rd size only:
Work as given for Back.

*** All sizes:
Cont in patt until Front measures 47cm (18½in) from beg,

ending with a WS row (end with a RS row here for Right front).

Shape armhole:

Cast/bind off 6 sts at beg of next row. Work 1 row. Dec 1 st at armhole edge on next 6 rows, then on every foll alt row until 29[37:41] sts rem. Work straight until Front is 27 rows (28 rows when working Right front) shorter than Back, ending at front edge.

Shape neck:

Cast/bind off 6[7:8] sts at beg of next row. Dec 1 st at neck edge on every row until 20[27:30] sts rem, then on every foll alt row until 17[24:27] sts rem and then on every foll 4th row until 14[21:24] sts rem. Patt 5 rows straight (patt 6 rows here for Right front). Cast/bind off.

RIGHT FRONT:

With 3.25mm (no. 10/US 3) needles cast on 49[57:61] sts. Work 7 rows in moss/seed st as given for Back.
Change to 4mm (no. 8/US 6) needles. Cont in lace patt as foll:

1st and 2nd sizes only:

Work as given for Back.

3rd size only:

1st row: (WS) P to end.
2nd row: K2, yo, sl 1, k1, psso, k1, *k2tog, yo, k3, yo, sl 1, k1, psso, k1, rep from * to end.
3rd row: P to end.
4th row: K2tog, *yo, k5, yo, sl 1, k2tog, psso, rep from * to last 3 sts, yo, k3.
Work as given for Left front from ** to **.

1st and 2nd sizes only:

1st row: (WS) P to end.
2nd row: K2, yo, sl 1, k1, psso, k1, *k2tog, yo, k3, yo, sl 1, k1, psso, k1, rep from * to end.
3rd row: P to end.
4th row: K2tog, *yo, k5, yo, sl 1, k2tog, psso, rep from * to last 3 sts, yo, k3.

3rd size only:

Work as given for Back.
Complete as given for Left front from *** to end, noting the bracketed exceptions.

SLEEVES: (Make 2)

With 3.25mm (no. 10/US 3) needles cast on 57[57:65] sts. Work 7 rows in moss/seed st as given for Back.
Change to 4mm (no. 8/US 6) needles. Cont in lace patt as given for Back, inc 1 st at each end of every foll 10th[8th:8th] row until there are 77[75:73] sts, then on every foll 12th[10th:10th] row until there are 79[83:89] sts. Cont without shaping until Sleeve measures 46[46:47] cm/18[18:18½]in from beg, ending with a WS row.

Shape top:

Cast/bind off 6 sts at beg of next 2 rows. Dec 1 st at each end of every row until 51[51:57] sts rem, then at each end of every foll alt row until 33[33:35] sts rem. Cast/bind off 3 sts at beg of next 6 rows. Cast/bind off rem 15[15:17] sts.

BUTTON BAND:

With 3.25mm (no. 10/US 3) needles cast on 7 sts. Cont in moss/seed st until band, when slight stretched, fits up Left front edge to beg of neck shaping. Cast/bind off.
Sew band in place on Left front edge. Mark positions of 8 buttons, the first 3 rows up from cast-on edge and the last 3 rows down from cast/bound-off edge, with the others evenly spaced between.

BUTTONHOLE BAND:

Work to match Button Band, making buttonholes as markers are reached as foll:
1st row: (RS) Patt 3 sts, work 2tog, patt 2 sts.
2nd row: Patt 3 sts, yo, patt 3 sts.

COLLAR:

Join shoulder seams.
With 3.25mm (no. 10/US 3) needles and RS of work facing, rejoin yarn to 4th st on buttonhole band, pick up and k 33[35:36] sts up right front neck, 3 sts down right back neck, k across 29[31:33] centre back neck sts on holder, pick up and k 3 sts up left back neck and 33[35:36] sts down left front neck to 4th st on button band. 101[107:111] sts. Cont in moss/seed st throughout, work 6 rows.
Change to 4mm (no. 8/US 6) needles. Work 12 rows straight, then a further 8 rows dec 1 st at each end of every row. Cut off yarn and leave rem 85[91:95] sts on a holder.

Edging:

With 4mm (no. 8/US 6) needles and RS of work facing, pick up and k21 sts along row ends of collar on left front, k across 85[91:95] sts from holder, then pick up and k 21 sts along row ends of collar on right front. 127[133:137] sts. K 1 row. Cast/bind off loosely knitwise.

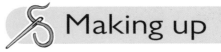 Making up

Sew in sleeves. Join side and sleeve seams.
Sew on buttons.

Zipped jacket

This really is a quick and easy knit that's ideal for the beginner and fantastic to wear once it's completed.

GETTING STARTED

Stitch pattern and shaping are easy for beginners to follow. Care must be taken to sew in the zip neatly

Size:

To fit bust: 81[86:91:97]cm/32[34:36:38]in

Actual size: 100[105:111:116]cm/39½[41½:43¾: 45¾]in

Length: 55[55:56:56]cm/21¾[21¾:22:22]in

Sleeve seam: 46[46:47:47]cm/18[18:18½:18½]in

Note: *Figures in square brackets [ ] refer to larger sizes; where there is only one set of figures, it applies to all sizes*

How much yarn:

15[16:17:18] x 50g (2oz) balls of Debbie Bliss Cashmerino Chunky, approx 65m (71 yards) per ball

Needles:

Pair of 6mm (no. 4/US 10) knitting needles

Pair of 7mm (no. 2/US 10½) knitting needles

Additional items:

56cm (22in) open-ended zip fastener

Stitch holders

Tension/gauge:

15 sts and 22 rows measure 10cm (4in) square over patt on 7mm (no. 2/US 10½) needles.

IT IS ESSENTIAL TO WORK TO THE STATED TENSION/GAUGE TO ACHIEVE SUCCESS

What you have to do:

Work in garter stitch (every row knit). Work in wide rib pattern. Work simple decreases for armhole and neck shaping. Work simple increases for sleeve shaping. Pick up stitches for collar and front bands. Sew in zip fastener.

Relax in this chunky casual jacket knitted in a wide-rib pattern with garter-stitch borders.

The Yarn

Luxuriously soft and thick, Debbie Bliss Cashmerino Chunky is a mixture of 55% merino wool with 33% microfibre and 12% cashmere. This weight is ideal for outer garments and is available in wide range of fashionable colours.

Abbreviations:

alt = alternate;
beg = beginning;
cm = centimetre(s);
cont = continue;
dec = decrease(ing);
foll = following;
g st = garter stitch
(every row knit);
inc = increase(ing);
k = knit; **p** = purl;
patt = pattern;
rem = remain(ing);
rep = repeat;
RS = right side;
st(s) = stitch(es);
tog = together;
WS = wrong side

Instructions

BACK:

With 6mm (no. 4/US 10) needles cast on 75[79:83:87] sts.
Work 6 rows in g st.
Change to 7mm (no. 2/US 10½) needles. Commence patt.
1st row: (RS) K to end.
2nd row: P1[3:1:3], *k1, p3, rep from * to last 2[4:2:4] sts,
k1, p1[3:1:3]. These 2 rows form patt. Cont in patt until
Back measures 33cm (13in) from beg, ending with a WS
row.

Shape armholes:

Cast/bind off 2 sts at beg of next 2 rows. Dec 1 st at each
end of next 3 rows, then at each end of foll 3 alt rows.
59[63:67:71] sts. Work straight until armholes measure
22[22:23:23]cm/8¾[8¾:9:9]in from beg, ending with a
WS row.

Shape shoulders:

Cast/bind off 6[6:7:7] sts at beg of next 4 rows and 5[7:6:8]
sts at beg of foll 2 rows. Cast/bind off rem 25[25:27:27] sts.

LEFT FRONT:

With 6mm (no. 4/US 10) needles cast on 38[40:42:44] sts.
Work 6 rows in g st.
Change to 7mm (no. 2/US 10½) needles. Commence patt.
1st row: (RS) K to end.
2nd row: *K1, p3, rep from * to last 2[4:2:4] sts, k1,
p1[3:1:3].
These 2 rows form patt. **Cont in patt until Left front
matches Back to armholes, ending with a WS row (for Right
front, end with a RS row here).

Shape armhole:

Cast/bind off 2 sts at beg of next row. Dec 1 st at armhole
edge on next 3 rows, then on foll 3 alt rows. 30[32:34:36]
sts. Work straight until there are 16[16:18:18] rows less than
Back to start of shoulder shaping, ending with a WS row.**

Shape neck:

Next row: Patt 23[25:27:29] sts, turn and leave rem
7 sts on a holder.
***Dec 1 st at neck edge on next 4 rows, then on foll
2[2:3:3] alt rows. 17[19:20:22] sts. Work 7 rows straight,
ending at armhole edge (for Right front, work
8 rows here).

Shape shoulder:

Cast/bind off 6[6:7:7] sts at beg of next and foll alt row.
Work 1 row. Cast/bind off rem 5[7:6:8] sts.

RIGHT FRONT:

With 6mm (no. 4/US 10) needles cast on 38[40:42:44]
sts. Work 6 rows in g st. Change to 7mm (no. 2/US 10½)
needles.
Commence patt.
1st row: (RS) K to end.
2nd row: P1[3:1:3], *k1, p3, rep from * to last st, k1.
These 2 rows form patt. Work as given for Left front from
** to **, noting the bracketed exception.

Shape neck:

Next row: Cut off yarn and slip first 7 sts on to a holder,
rejoin yarn to rem 23[25:27:29] sts and patt to end.

BEGINNERS' STITCH GUIDE

WIDE RIB

This jacket is knitted in an easy-to-follow wide rib pattern. The edge of the jacket has a garter-stitch band consisting of six knit rows. The rib pattern is then formed from knitting the first row, which is the right side. Begin the second row with a number

of purl stitches (as specified in pattern), then repeat a sequence of knit 1, purl 3, across the row, ending as specified. These two rows form the pattern.

Complete as given for Left front from *** to end, noting the bracketed exception.

SLEEVES: (Make 2)

With 6mm (no. 4/US 10) needles cast on 41[41:43:43] sts.
Work 6 rows in g st.
Change to 7mm (no. 2/US 10½) needles.
Commence patt.
1st row: (RS) K to end.
2nd row: P2[2:3:3], *k1, p3, rep from * to last 3[3:4:4] sts, k1, p2[2:3:3].
These 2 rows form patt. Cont in patt, inc 1 st at each end of 5th and every foll 6th row until there are 51[51:57:57] sts, then on every foll 8th row until there are 65[65:69:69] sts, working extra sts into patt.
Work straight until Sleeve measures 46[46:47:47] cm/18[18:18½:18½]in from beg, ending with a WS row.

Shape top:

Cast/bind off 2 sts at beg of next 8 rows, then 3 sts at beg of foll 4 rows. Cast/bind off rem 37[37:41:41] sts.

COLLAR:

Join shoulder seams.
With 6mm (no. 4/US 10) needles and RS of work facing, k7 sts from Right front holder, pick up and k16[16:18:18] sts up right front neck, 23[23:25:25] sts across back neck, 16[16:18:18] sts down left front neck, then k7 sts from Left front holder. 69[69:75:75] sts.
Work 11 rows in g st, ending with a WS row.
Next row: (RS) K4[4:3:3], k2tog, (k5, k2tog, k6, k2tog) 4 times, (k5, k2tog) 0[0:1:1] time, k3. 60[60:65:65] sts.
Cont in g st until Collar measures 8cm (3in), ending with a RS row. Cast/bind off.

LEFT FRONT BORDER:

With 6mm (no.4/US 10) needles and RS of work facing, start at cast/bound-off edge of Collar and pick up and k80 sts along Left front opening edge, ending at cast-on edge. Cast/bind off knitways.

RIGHT FRONT BORDER:

With 6mm (no. 4/US 10) needles and RS of work facing, start at cast-on edge and pick up and k80 sts along Right front opening edge, ending at cast/bound-off edge of Collar. Cast/bind off knitways.

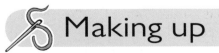

Making up

Press work carefully, following instructions on ball band and avoiding g st sections.
Sew in sleeves, placing centre of cast/bound-off edge of sleeves to shoulder seams. Join side and sleeve seams.
Sew in zip fastener.

Index

Acknowledgements

Managing Editor: Clare Churly
Editors: Jane Ellis and Sarah Hoggett
Senior Art Editor: Juliette Norsworthy
Designer: Janis Utton
Production Controller: Sarah Kramer